WHAT IS YOUR PLAN B?

A COACH CAPTAIN'S COMMENTARY OF THE BIBLE

JOHN CRONSHAW

Ark House Press
PO Box 1722, Port Orchard, WA 98366 USA
PO Box 1321, Mona Vale NSW 1660 Australia
PO Box 318 334, West Harbour, Auckland 0661 New Zealand
arkhousepress.com

© John Cronshaw 2020

All rights reserved. No part of this publication may be reproduced, stored in a retrieval system or transmitted in any form or by any means electronic, mechanical, photocopying, recording or otherwise without the prior written permission of the publisher.

Scripture quotations are from the New Revised Standard Version Bible, copyright © 1989 National Council of the Churches of Christ in the United States of America. Used by permission. All rights reserved worldwide.

Cataloguing in Publication Data:
Title: What Is Your Plan B?
ISBN: 978-0-6488259-0-6 (pbk)
Subjects: Christian Living;

Design by initiateagency.com

CONTENTS

Introduction v

Dedication: ix

Let's Get Started. xi

God's Plan A 1

Promises And Prophecies 17

Emmanuel – God With Us 49

The "Lost Years" 63

Three Short Years 79

Three Short Weeks 107

Three Long Days 137

The Rest Of Time 155

Postscript – P.S. 171

Other Books From John Cronshaw: 175

GOD'S PLAN A

INTRODUCTION

As a Coach Captain for more than forty years, my role in running a tour was to offer a commentary on the places we visited. The training document stated that a commentary was something that was to educate and inform in an interesting way so one would undertake research through reading of the places visited, and then condense the information into something that was educational and interesting. Because people were on holidays, they did not need to have a detailed background given to them, so the job of editing the background information was an important task.

I have been a Christian since I gave my heart to the Lord back in 1960, and apart from a lot of reading and a small amount of part-time study, (a course called the SPTC) I have had no formal theological training. This book is heavily edited to make the Bible story readable and I trust, interesting. You can buy large volumes of Bible Commentaries with numerous cross-references and extensive bibliographies. Bookshops have shelves of very extensive commentaries of every book of the Bible. This book does not serve to repeat these volumes, nor compete with them.

In the forty or so years I have been driving tours, I have also been operating Christian tours where each day we held a short devotional talk.

This was categorized as 'One Verse – One Thought'. Previously I have published a book of these devotions, *Buspa's Corner* and also produced a CD *Moving Devotions with Buspa*. (I am the Grandpa with the buses)

This small book has an interesting birth. It was a small, casual gathering for worship in a small church called Auburn Hub where I was to speak. It wasn't really a sermon; that's not how they have church. It was to be more conversational. My plan was to speak about the greatest temptation we face (to give up our faith – that comes later) and the Bible reading was from Luke 22:39-46.

Luke 22:39-46 (NRSV)

Jesus Prays on the Mount of Olives

39 He came out and went, as was his custom, to the Mount of Olives; and the disciples followed him. **40** When he reached the place, he said to them, "Pray that you may not come into the time of trial." **41** Then he withdrew from them about a stone's throw, knelt down, and prayed, **42** "Father, if you are willing, remove this cup from me; yet, not my will but yours be done." **43** Then an angel from heaven appeared to him and gave him strength. **44** In his anguish he prayed more earnestly, and his sweat became like great drops of blood falling down on the ground. **45** When he got up from prayer, he came to the disciples and found them sleeping because of grief, **46** and he said to them, "Why are you sleeping? Get up and pray that you may not come into the time of trial."

These verses were read and Darren, my son and pastor, then invited people to chat about these verses before I was to lead the group. My intention was to emphasise the last phrase, "Get up and pray that you may not come into the time of trial." The NIV translation uses the term 'temptation'. "Get up and pray so that you will not fall into temptation."

The group had another emphasis: they focused in on the few lines before my selected verse "found them sleeping because of grief". The NIV speaks of 'exhausted from sorrow.'

We asked the question, why were the disciples "exhausted from sorrow," or what was their grief? On the night before the Crucifixion chain of events, they hadn't experienced that sorrow or grief. Why would they be "exhausted from sorrow" on this night before the Passover?

And so began my walk backwards through time; from the Garden of Gethsemane to the week before, (eight days actually) then tracing the walk undertaken by Jesus that led to Jerusalem via Bethany, Jericho, the Mount of Transfiguration, Capernaum and Caesarea Philippi. Come with me as we walk with Jesus and His disciples in the condensed few weeks leading to the very reason, God's Plan A, a plan that saw Jesus praying in the Garden of Gethsemane on the Mount of Olives that night.

DEDICATION:

This book is dedicated to the many people whose path I have crossed in my life's faith walk – too many to mention by name, and many unknown to me who played an integral part in my journey

People who prayed for me, who encouraged me to go to church, who encouraged me when giving talks and devotions with a pat on the back or a "that was helpful" comment.

As one looks back over one's pathway in life, little points stand out in memory of the positive impact people have played in my life. I thank God for those people and I pray that I may also be a little link in the chain that eternally encourages another pilgrim on the way.

John Cronshaw

January 2020

LET'S GET STARTED.

On the back of taxis and buses in Sydney, we have seen advertising to "Make this bus your Plan B" for those who wish to have a night out and may be over the alcohol driving limit. I am making an assumption: your life that you are leading (or have been leading) is one that you would describe as your own Plan A, but there may have been (or are) aspects of your life that you wish to change. My assumption here is that your current Plan A for your life, if you want to change it, becomes your new Plan B. Yet your Plan B is really God's Plan A and has been from the beginning.

I find when I am reading a book like this that sometimes you find there are too many Bible references, so you don't pause to read any of them. Or when they are printed, you tend to skip through them. In this book about God's Plan A, I have recorded the full set of Bible verses in the text of the book so that you don't have to pause and look for the references. In some situations, where the extra Bible readings will be a help to a greater understanding but they don't add anything specific to what I am writing, I have listed the references. You may elect to stop to read these, or mark them to read later.

My intention in writing *God's Plan A* is not to present another academic study of the Bible – there are plenty of those available. My life's career has been that of a coach captain in my own business, and as such part of the tour experience is to give the passengers a commentary on the places we visit. Because passengers are on holidays, they want to find out things about where we are, but they don't want to sit for an examination at the end. That means in my commentary I have made an effort to present the details in an interesting manner, and aimed to link the places we visited with other aspects of Australian geography, history and landforms.

The tours we offer also include a tour to Jordan and Israel that is called "The Land of the Bible". To greatly assist our passengers in understanding more of the "why" than the "where" and "when" of this amazing part of the world, the book "Land of the Bible" has been published. It also is written in an interesting but simplified way, linking as best I could the historical aspects of the Land of the Bible with God's intention in the enactment of His Story. In some ways, this book "God's Plan A" has grown out of our tours into the Land of the Bible. It stands alone, but it also makes a great companion guide to any person wanting to enjoy a sightseeing tour of Jordan and Israel.

Most importantly, my prayer is that you will be blessed by your reading and it is one link in the chain that forms your spiritual walk with the Living Lord.

John Cronshaw
Bonny Hills, NSW, Australia.
January 2020

CHAPTER 1

GOD'S PLAN A

I do not know how old the Earth is. I do not know how long people have lived on Earth. There are some things back then that I cannot really get a handle on. Now, before you start telling me that the Earth is X years old, or before you tell me there is a Creation Science timeline I can extrapolate backwards. Before you say there are rocks on earth that are calculated to be Y years old, I am asking you not to place a figure on the age of the Earth, or the age of human habitation. When our minister wanted to do a short series on Science and Religion he asked for some comments from people, and one person said something to the effect of, "I am not sure of the actual times or the processes used in creation and I have them put aside to one day ask God about them. What I do believe is that God made the heavens and the earth and people as He states in the Bible."

Evolution, Creation Science, The Big Bang. So many words have been written over the years about these things and each generation brings with it discoveries and theories either intending to support the Bible or to discredit it. One only has to look at microbiology, organic chemistry and what is known about atomic structure, the intricacies of the DNA molecule (the understanding of which is only a couple of generations old) to marvel at the natural world. As astrophysics sends probes into the solar system, so new stars and planets are discovered and the dimensions of the 'known' universe must make us understand our relative smallness in the astronomical scheme of the universe.

Just come back in time with me (and I don't know if time travel is possible, but humour me a little) and we need to go back a long time. On the time scale of things, as we go back, we come to people, then nature, then the Earth, then the Heavens, along with light and dark. We will come back to the time when people first appeared on this time line, but before anything existed at all, there was a void. There was no matter. It was a void. There was nothing.

Except God.

God.

"An invisible spirit that is Infinite, Eternal and Unchangeable, in His being, wisdom, power, holiness, justice, goodness and truth."[1]

Because God is Eternal, it means He has always existed and will always exist. He is timeless. If you think that is a hard concept to grasp,

The Christian "fish" symbol comes from the Greek word ICHTHYS which means fish, but it was also taken to be the acrostic for Jesus Christ Son of God Saviour ("Ἰησοῦς Χριστός, Θεοῦ Υἱός, Σωτήρ», (Iēsous Christos, Theou Yios, Sōtēr)

---

1 *A Body of Divinity*. Thomas Watson. First published 1692 *The Banner of Truth Trust*. A Catechism style teaching.

you are right. It is impossible to understand this because we have a timeline, a beginning and an earthly end. Try to imagine this situation of God as a triune God, the God of the Trinity, of God the Father, God the Son and God the Holy Spirit co-existing before Creation was Created with a word. Read Genesis Chapter 1 and you will pick this up: "And God said…" Psalm 33:6 states: "By the word of the Lord the heavens were made, and all their host by the breath of his mouth."

After God created the heavens and the earth. When the earth was fit and able to support human habitation, "Then God said, 'Let us make humankind in our image, according to our likeness; Let us make man in our image.'" (Genesis 1:26-31 to read it all).

The Bible is a love letter from God. It is a book that records the inter-relationship between God as Creator and Humankind as the created. In a chicken and egg situation, obviously Jesus came first and mankind second, but I want to spend just a little time writing about you. You are important to you, and you are important to God. In the Devotion in this Chapter, I write what I claim to be the Bible in a sentence. God speaking says, "John (my name – insert your name), I love you because I made you. I want to spend Eternity with you, and I want your life to reflect this."

What God says about you:

You are created by God in the image of God. "Let us make humankind in our image…" (Genesis 1:26) This word "image" could be a stumbling block to your understanding, but by 'image', the Bible does not refer to something like a photographic image. God is a spirit and as such is invisible, but He has characteristics and character attributes such as love, wisdom, justice and goodness. Being made in His image means that we also have these character attributes built in to our nature.

You have been fearfully and wonderfully made. Psalm 139 verses 13 to 16 are beautiful words from God to encourage you of your relationship with the Creator of all things:

> For it was you who formed my inward parts;
>   you knit me together in my mother's womb.
> I praise you, for I am fearfully and wonderfully made.
>   Wonderful are your works;
> that I know very well.
> My frame was not hidden from you,
> when I was being made in secret,
>   intricately woven in the depths of the earth.
> Your eyes beheld my unformed substance.
> In your book were written
>   all the days that were formed for me,
>   when none of them as yet existed."

Note the last verse quoted: God has written in His book your days before any days came to be. Before He created anything, He has planned your life's days and they have been planned since before the beginning of time!

God knows you intimately and by name.

"But now thus says the Lord, he who created you, O Jacob, he who formed you, O Israel: Do not fear, for I have redeemed you; I have called you by name, you are mine." (Isaiah 43:1)

God's knowledge of you is intimate. "But even the hairs of your head are all counted. Do not be afraid; you are of more value than many sparrows." (Luke 12:7)

You are special; you are unique. You are loved by God. This story of the Bible is about you and your precious relationship with God, who created you and who gives you life and breath.

What God says about Jesus

Before humankind was created in God's image, before any matter with any form or substance was created by God's breath, Jesus, as an integral part of the Godhead, existed. Before Adam and Eve, before the Garden of Eden, Jesus existed as a part of the Godhead. Please think about this for a minute; ponder awhile or meditate, if that helps.

While you are meditating on this, perhaps a few Bible verses may be useful to add to the mix. The Gospel of John, and Colossians Chapter 1 explain the importance of Jesus in God's Plan A: His purposes.

John 1:1-5 | The Word Became Flesh

"In the beginning was the Word, and the Word was with God, and the Word was God. He was in the beginning with God. All things came into being through him, and without him not one thing came into being. What has come into being in him was life, and the life was the light of all people. The light shines in the darkness, and the darkness did not overcome it."

Colossians 1:15-20 | The Supremacy of the Son of God

"He is the image of the invisible God, the firstborn of all creation; for in him all things in heaven and on earth were created, things visible and invisible, whether thrones or dominions or rulers or powers—all things have been created through him and for him. He himself is before all things, and in him all things hold together. He is the head of the body, the church; he is the beginning, the firstborn from the dead, so that he might come to have first place in everything. For in him all the fullness of God was pleased to dwell, and through him God was pleased to reconcile to himself all things, whether on earth or in heaven, by making peace through the blood of his cross."

Apologies if you think I am labouring the point, but it is an important point to grasp.

Before any creation.

Before human creation.

Before Adam and Eve and the sin in the Garden of Eden.

However long that period of time, Jesus was God's Plan A. Adam and Eve's sin in the Garden of Eden did not catch God short. Because He is all knowing, (omniscient) He knew that the jewel of His creation – humankind – would be evicted from His presence and the history of humankind from that day on until The Annunciation would be the focus of God to reconcile us, the jewel of His creation, to Himself.

The Bible is His Story. It is historical, but it is not just a history book. It is a narrow sliver of human history independent of the whole of human history. It is God's Plan A being enacted through an amazingly detailed record of God's dealing with one man – Abram – through to the coming to live on Earth in Divine mystery of God's Son – God – in the form of Jesus. Please slowly read the few verses I have repeated above and envelope your thoughts around this important fact. Try if you can to put this into a timeline to scale.

Before anything was created, we have God and Jesus. (Now that is impossible to put to a scale because there is no scale possible, so we have to start with some dotted line.)

There is a creation of the Heavens and the Earth and the life on Earth. (Probably possible to get a scale but not a real, accurate scale – just a lot of line.)

Humankind is created. Adam and Eve's life recorded; banishment from the Garden of Eden.

From the Bible, we can start to get a timescale with some ages recorded: Noah and his sons through to Abram / Abraham. Then we have a timescale that starts to have a meaning, we can understand as we live through the lives of Isaac, Jacob and Israel. Then the 400 years of slavery in Egypt, the Exodus, 40 years of wilderness wanderings. Joshua and the conquests of the Promised Land follows, the period of the Judges, King Saul, King David and then through the exile of the Israelites to Babylon and their tumultuous history of obedience / disobedience. God speaking through the prophets ("Long ago God spoke to our ancestors in many and various ways by the prophets." Hebrews 1:1) all had a common message that pointed to the coming of a Messiah: one who would deliver them.

If your personality needs to be accurate on this timeline, then you can easily get copies of the period of time I have written about, but my emphasis is not on the detail of the time, but rather to make an observation. In human history terms, it was a long time. In earth history, universe timing, it is relatively short.

As we look back on this very brief summary, we need to be reminded that we are looking back with the benefit of hindsight, knowing full well the results that followed. The people whose lives are recorded in the Bible did not have this hindsight of history, so we need to try to understand their position and their reactions to the circumstances.

And it is to twelve people, twelve ordinary people, to whom we turn to put ourselves in their shoes as they walked a very short distance for a very short time with this person who was and is still, God's Plan A for you and for me... and for all people. He assures us that, "The Lord is not slow about his promise, as some think of slowness, but is patient with you, **not wanting any to perish**, but all to come to repentance." (2 Peter 3:9 – emphasis mine)

So what exactly is God's Plan A?

You may have heard the statement 'The Gospel is the good news'. There are four books called Gospels in the beginning of the New Testament. Are these part of the story?

The word gospel has a Greek origin and it means good news. In classical Greek, the word designated the reward given for good tidings and also included the message itself. The book of the Gospel of Mark starts with the words, "The beginning of the good news of Jesus Christ, the Son of God." The NIV records "The beginning of the gospel about Jesus Christ, the Son of God." (Mark 1:1) The books, the Gospels, record the story of Jesus Christ – his birth, his ministry of teaching, the working of miracles, his voluntary death, resurrection and ascension and the prophecy of his return to Earth at some distant time unknown to any but God. It also features how the coming of Jesus, as God's plan A, is the fulfillment of many prophecies made well in advance of the event during historical periods of the Children of Israel, the Jewish nation.

So well may we ask, "Why did Jesus come to Earth, and why did He have to die?"

It seems to be a long, drawn out process spread over four thousand years or so in the 21st century as we look back to the time of Abraham and it seems to be such a complicated concept. Let me state at the outset: the Christian faith is the only faith or religion in the world that has been initiated and enacted by the God whom we worship. It is not 'manmade', although God used many people in His service and in the writing of the books of the Bible. My starting point and reference point is the statement, "The Bible is what it says it is, and God is who He says He is in the Bible."

Before I start, let me pause for some help. Because we are dealing with very important things about God, He promises to help us in our understanding through His Holy Spirit, so if this is the first time you have come across the summary of the Gospel, please pray a prayer and ask God to help you in your understanding.

> *Dear God, as I start to read about the Gospel of the Lord Jesus Christ, I pray that your Holy Spirit will soften my heart to the things of God, and help me to understand the things I read. Amen.*

The Beginning

The Bible starts, "In the beginning when God created the heavens and the earth." (Genesis 1:1) In the Biblical account of creation, we read in Genesis 1: 26 "Then God said, 'Let us make humankind in our image, according to our likeness; and let them have dominion over the fish of the sea, and over the birds of the air, and over the cattle, and over all the wild animals of the earth, and over every creeping thing that creeps upon the earth.' So God created humankind in his image, in the image of God he created them; male and female he created them."

In verse 31 we read, "God saw everything that he had made, and indeed, it was very good. And there was evening and there was morning, the sixth day." It is an important thing to notice and believe "the Lord God formed man from the dust of the ground, and breathed into his nostrils the breath of life; and the man became a living being." (Genesis 2:7)

We move in this Genesis account to the Garden of Eden. (Genesis 2:8) In verse 16 we read, " And the Lord God commanded the man, "You may freely eat of every tree of the garden; but of the tree of the knowledge of good and evil you shall not eat, for in the day that you eat of it you shall die."

I recommend to you that you read Genesis Chapters 1 through to the end of Chapter 3 to gain a fuller understanding of this situation. Note the word "commanded" when God spoke to Adam about living in the Garden that God created and provided for their living – a garden that, along with all of creation, God saw that it was good.

For a sense of understanding God's authority as creator, turn with me to Exodus Chapter 20 to read of how God issued the Ten Commandments. Note the word "commandment" again. These Ten Commandments start with the first that states, very clearly and categorically, "Then God spoke all these words: I am the Lord your God, who brought you out of the land of Egypt, out of the house of slavery; you shall have no other gods before me."

The first step in understanding the Gospel of Jesus Christ is the need to accept God's place in our life and that is as Lord of our life. These few verses give that sense of authority.

Job 33:4

"The Spirit of God has made me, and the breath of the Almighty gives me life."

Isaiah 42:5

"Thus says God the LORD, Who created the heavens and stretched them out, Who spread out the earth and what comes from it, who gives breath to the people upon it and spirit to those who walk in it."

Acts 17:25

"… nor is He served by human hands, as though He needed anything, since He Himself gives to all mortals life and breath and all things."

God's initial and original plan for humankind was that we were made in the image of God in order that the Creator of the Universe could have fellowship with and communicate with the jewel of His creation. This plan was marred by Adam and Eve's disobedience because they were tempted and tricked by the serpent – more crafty than any of the wild animals the Lord God had made. This disobedience is called sin.

Let me warn you (or encourage you): the term *sin* is not a very popular term today. The term's origin in Hebrew or Greek refers to missing the mark, or deviating from the goal, rebellion or revolution, taking a wrong road or the violation of God's law. I might suggest that when we break the first commandment or violate God's command to have no other gods but the God of the Bible, the other actions that could be construed as sinful all follow more easily. Looking at some of the definitions above, you may pick up that some actions like missing the mark may come about with a different motivation or attitude in our heart and mind than others such as rebellion. Many people like to grade sin and consider some sinful actions as worse than others, but this is not what the Bible teaches.

The history of the Israelites, from Abraham through to Jesus, is really a history of the ups and downs of a group of people in their relationship with God and their attitude to Him. Turning to the New Testament to the first chapter of the Book of Romans (Romans 1:18-25) we read a summary of God's wrath against mankind because of their willful disobedience, their rebellion and revolution – their sin.

The Guilt of Humankind

"For the wrath of God is revealed from heaven against all ungodliness and wickedness of those who, by their wickedness, suppress the truth. For what can be known about God is plain to them, because God has shown it to them. Ever since the creation of the world his eternal power and divine nature, invisible though they are, have been understood and seen through the things he has made. So they are without excuse; for though they knew God, they did not honour him as God or give thanks to him, but they became futile in their thinking, and their senseless minds were darkened. Claiming to be wise, they became fools; and they exchanged the glory of the immortal God for images resembling a mortal human being or birds or four-footed animals or reptiles.

"Therefore God gave them up in the lusts of their hearts to impurity, to the degrading of their bodies among themselves, because they exchanged the truth about God for a lie and worshiped and served the creature rather than the Creator, who is blessed forever! Amen."

I mentioned that some have the tendency to classify sins into big sins and little sins – some are worse than others. The Bible addresses this problem. James 2:10 states, "For whoever keeps the whole law falls at one point has become accountable for all of it." In Romans 3:23 we read, "Since all have sinned and fall short of the glory of God…"

As with Adam and Eve's banishment from the Garden of Eden because of their disobedience to God, so we also have the same penalty to face – banishment from God. Romans 6:23 is very clear as to the penalty for sin, but it is also clear about the solution.

"For the wages of sin is death, but the free gift of God is eternal life in Christ Jesus our Lord."

In summary so far –

- We have all sinned against God. We were born sinners – that is the natural, fallen, state of humankind. We sin because we are sinful.
- God is very clear: the penalty for sinning is banishment from his presence – death. Hebrews 9:27: "And just as it is appointed for mortals to die once, and after that the judgment."
- The "good news" is: "But the free gift of God is eternal life in Christ Jesus our Lord." (Romans 6:23)
- John 1:10-13 states: "He was in the world, and the world came into being through him; yet the world did not know him. He came to what was his own, and his own people did not accept him. But to all who received him, who believed in his name, he gave power to become children of God, who were born, not of blood or of the will of the flesh or of the will of man, but of God."

For the remainder of this book, we will be unpacking more and more of this gracious plan of God towards us as sinful people. My encouragement to you is to keep reading and keep praying that God's Holy Spirit will reveal more and more of His precious truths to you as you read and think on these things. The Postscript at the end of the book outlines how you can have peace with God and restore the original fellowship that God intended for you and your life.

Why would God bother? I have taken the liberty of reproducing a devotion from my book *'Buspa's Corner'* on this concept.

Why Bother?

For God so loved the world that he gave his only Son, so that everyone who believes in him may not perish but have eternal life.

John 3:16

While waiting around the school playground for my grandchildren to come out of school, I could not help overhear the conversations of mothers as school wound down for the year. The planning for Christmas dinners, the shopping for Christmas presents, the scheduling of having to meet with people for the never-ending round of Christmas drinks and functions.

Then suddenly, it is all over. Christmas presents are unwrapped at the speed of light, leaving a swathe of torn paper across the lounge room floor. A lunch that has taken weeks to plan, hours or days to prepare is suddenly a pile of dirty dishes.

Why bother?

As we think of Emmanuel, God with us, we need to be reminded that Jesus is and always was God's PLAN A. Pause to read John 1 and Colossians 1:15 and you will see it is very clear that Jesus was a part of the Godhead during Creation. He has always been and was never something that God needed to resort to when Adam and Eve were banished from His presence.

When we look at the creation of the world, all living things and the wonderful set of conditions that sustain life, including modern life, and pause to think of the time and intricate planning that God put into our creation, we could also ask the same question:

Why bother?

God, knowing the end from the beginning, knew that sinfulness would mar His creation and His plans for us. He knew that there would be a time in history when Jesus would leave the Godhead to live on Earth as a human. He knew that there would be a horrible period of time when Jesus would be separated from the Godhead as He paid the required penalty for our sin.

Why bother?

You would all have different, yet similar answers, why you bothered with Christmas preparations. The similarity possibly based on love for your family and the recipients of your gifts.

God's answer?

Because He loved us all that He gave His only Son so that we might believe, and having believed, be able to spend eternity with Him. Our devotion starts with John 3:16.

I summarise the Bible in one sentence: "John, I love you because I made you, I want to spend eternity with you, and I want your life to reflect this."

Thank God that He did bother to meticulously plan creation, that He sustains this creation and that out of love for each of us, He initiated an amazing, gracious plan that will ensure we who believe will be able to spend eternity with Him and with those whom we love who share that belief.

Thank you God that you did bother.

Prayer*: Thank you, dear Lord, that you did bother because of your love for us. Thank you that you took the time to plan the universe and all aspects of creation that you planned for Jesus to come to earth to make the pathway back to you a possibility and that you have planned a life for me.*

CHAPTER 2

PROMISES AND PROPHECIES

This is a tall order.

I am going to summarise the Old Testament of the Bible into just one chapter to explain how God's Plan A was to be enacted. This means one of two things will happen: either your head will spin, or you will be disappointed in its brevity. Please don't be disappointed by the brevity. There are numerous books written by wonderful authors and theologians who can fill in the many blanks. If your head is spinning after this, then perhaps you may like to stop for a while and think through what is written. It is important that we grasp the purpose of the Old Testament, for once the details of God's activity have been recorded, there is no need to re-write them again as we look at the content in the twenty first century. The lessons learned are timeless.

If you are a fan of cryptic crosswords, then much of what you read will be right up your alley. Remember at all times that we are reading everything through twenty first century eyes, so we have a big advantage over those early readers. The people living around the time of Jesus had great difficulty understanding everything they saw and heard, and for many, the texts would have been familiar to them. Be encouraged as you learn these things of God that, like all forms of learning, it is a process. However, our learning process is greatly enhanced by the gift of the Holy Spirit, so each time you approach God's Word, ensure that you pray and ask for the Holy Spirit's guidance and enlightenment. (Pray the prayer on page 9).

Before walking through the Bible, it may be helpful to explain a few terms that appear frequently and which may have some strong meanings attached, meanings that you may find offensive or cruel. We are living in a politically correct age where it is often difficult (or illegal) to state something that once was accepted as either fact or open for discussion. Because I am writing about God, my starting point is this:

"The Bible is what it says it is, and God is who He says He is in the Bible."

We have to sit on one side of the fence or the other. Either I believe in God, the God of the Bible, or I don't believe. For every human on earth, that is a simple choice and I need to say that I don't think there are any half measures.

Believe or don't believe.

Have faith or don't have faith.

Aim to live according to the Bible's tenets, or live a life that is free and easy, with no constraints.

Unapologetically, the purpose of this book is to trace the pathway of Jesus through the Bible to the last few weeks of his life, so it should come as no surprise that I am of the belief, faith, behaviour side of the argument. It is my choice to be one of God's people and I choose to believe that the God of the Bible is my God. So what are the terms about which I am speaking and with which I have taken some time to set the scene for discussion?

Messiah – We are well acquainted with the Operatic Oratorio composed by Handel – Handel's Messiah, and we hear Jesus often referred to as The Messiah. The term comes from military parlance and it means the liberation of a country or its people. The term is used as the official title of the central figure of the Jewish expectation of being liberated from Roman occupation, but it is a late term product of use, and is not used in the Old Testament.

There were Messianic expectations that according to prophecies, a deliverer would be raised up to deliver God's chosen people.

Anointed or Anointing – This term is used in the Old Testament and in historical records where it is suggested that certain Kings were appointed to accommodate a redemptive purpose towards God's people and a judgment on their foes. Anointing of persons or things with oil was will to signify holiness and to consecrate the person or thing.

Jesus - The name Jesus means "Saviour". It is the same name as Joshua in the Old Testament and it is given to our Lord because *"He will save His people from their sins."* (Matthew 1:21) This name was given to Mary when she was advised that she would bear the child. (Luke 1:31)

Christ – The term Christ originates from the Greek Christos and that means "Messiah", or "anointed one".

Redeemer – Redemption. Redemption means deliverance from some evil by the payment of a price.

Saviour – In general terms is a person who rescues another from danger. In Christian terms, when referring to Jesus as Saviour, it is specifically rescuing people from their sin.

Prophet – A person who speaks through divine inspiration and who may predict the future. A prophecy is a message of divine truth revealing God's will.

Vassal / Treaties – Particularly in times of war a conquering nation may subdue the vanquished and that group then becomes known as a Vassal State. Treaties are drawn up with legal rights and obligations that bind the Vassal State to the Conquering Nation. This treaty could also be referred to as a covenant. Today there is a space treaty between nations, with legal obligations imposed on the countries shooting satellites into space.

Covenant – A binding law or agreement in writing and under seal that commits parties to the agreement on both sides. God's covenant with His chosen people usually was for Lordship: "No other gods but me" and His promises were predicated on these covenants.

Testament – From Greek origins, the New Testament treatment of the word covenant is taken from the Greek word for 'testament'.

Gospel – Of Greek origin meaning "good news". In classical literature, the word was for the reward given for good tidings, originally the announcement of victory. In the NT it is mentioned 75 times, giving the term a distinctly Christian connotation. The term is both the book and the story. Mark 16:15-16: "And he said to them, 'Go into all the world and proclaim the good news to the whole creation. The one who believes and is baptized will be saved; but the one who does not believe will be condemned.'"

There are other terms we find in the Bible, many of which are not acceptable today as "politically correct". Society seems to be in a furore over their use and the terminology. It is important that we look at these terms and understand their meaning, as a lawyer would say, "without prejudice", and as I write I also state without judgment.

In reading these definitions and examples of the commonly used terms, it is important that you apply them to your own life and circumstances. They are not intended to classify other people. In the words of the prophet Elijah, when he squared off against the prophets of Baal on Mount Carmel, "How long will you go limping with two different opinions? If the LORD is God, follow him; but if Baal, then follow him." And the people did not answer him a word." (1 Kings 18:21)

Everyone has a choice when it comes to belief and relationship to God – choose God or reject God. The following terms parallel this decision.

Fool / Foolish – A person who lacks sense or judgment. "Fools say in their hearts, 'There is no God.' They are corrupt, their do abominable deeds; there is no one who does good." (Psalm 14:1) The world regards Christians as fools, (1 Cor 4:10) but the Bible tells us that fools do not believe in God, (Psalm 53:1) they do not trust God, (Psalm 92:6) they act in a godless manner, (Psalm 94:5-8) they are dishonest, (Jeremiah 17:11) they are disobedient (Psalm 107:17) and they despise instruction and discipline. (Proverbs 1:28-33)

Wise / Wisdom – Prudent, sensible, prompted by wisdom or discernment. The ability to think, act and utilize knowledge, showing common sense and insight. "The fear of the LORD **is the beginning of wisdom, and knowledge of the Holy One is** insight." (Proverbs 9:10) Biblical wisdom is both religious and practical, stemming from the fear of the Lord.

Blessed – A common OT word when used for man denotes a sense of happiness, and when applied to God has a sense of praise. Happy are those who do not follow the advice of the wicked, or take the path that sinners tread, or sit in the seat of scoffers." (Psalm 1:1) The NIV states, "Blessed is the one…" The term is given a strong spiritual content as revealed in the Beatitudes from The Sermon on the Mount. (Matthew 5:3-11)

Cursed – There are two aspects to this term. We read of something or someone being cursed by another and we read of the state of a person being cursed. A person could utter a curse, desiring another's hurt. God's curse is usually a denunciation of sin and his judgment on sin. There is a relationship between obedience and blessing, disobedience and cursing. For God's curse to fall on disobedient people, it really is the implementation of the terms of His covenant.

Wicked – Means morally bad, troublesome, unpleasant or offensive. In the Bible the terms are connected with ungodly and evil. Wickedness has its seat in the heart and is inspired by Satan. "And he said, "It is what comes out of a person that defiles. For it is from within, from the human heart, that evil intentions come: fornication, theft, murder." (Mark 7:20-21)

Righteous – The term comes from an Arab root meaning "straightness". It has two connections: one being people to people and the other between people and God. Between people it is "right living" that leads to better community. In dealing with God, it implies a correct relationship with God, being "right" with God, and it is here that we need to understand that, with God, His righteousness is a part of the character of God, along with His holiness. Isaiah 64:6 states, "All our righteous deeds are like a filthy cloth" and we read that, "Abram believed the Lord, and the Lord reckoned it to him as righteousness." (Genesis 15:6) 2 Corinthians 5:21 is a pivotal verse to understand: "For our sake he made him (Jesus) to be sin who knew no sin, so that in him we might become the righteousness of God."

Heaven – God's habitation where he is worshipped and served by angels. Very little is written describing the "geography" of heaven, but in summary, it could be called a place where we will be with God.

Psalm 11:4: "The Lord is in his holy temple; the Lord's throne is in heaven. His eyes behold, his gaze examines humankind."

Hell – The place of eternal punishment in fire and darkness intended for Satan and those who choose to reject God. Matthew 13:40-42: "Just as the weeds are collected and burned up with fire, so will it be at the end of the age. The Son of Man will send his angels, and they will collect out of his kingdom all causes of sin and all evildoers, and they will throw them into the furnace of fire, where there will be weeping and gnashing of teeth."

Eternal Life – The state of being in a permanent, never-ending relationship with God with a unique quality of life, knowing that the source is God himself. This is the critical part of God's covenant, the end result of His Plan A through Jesus Christ. The assurance of Eternal Life comes with it the assurance of our bodily resurrection. Psalm 16:11: "You show me the path of life. In your presence there is fullness of joy; in your right hand are pleasures forevermore."

Eternal Judgment – For many, this concept is a huge stumbling block. The question is often asked, "If God is a God of love, how could he let people go into hell for the rest of time?" The reality is that Eternal separation from God is a consequence of un-repented sin. It is a consequence of one turning one's back on the God who gives life, but who has offered Eternal Life through Jesus Christ. "And just as it is appointed for mortals to die once, and after that the judgment, so Christ, having been offered once to bear the sins of many, will appear a second time, not to deal with sin, but to save those who are eagerly waiting for him." (Hebrews 9:27-28)

The Word of God

In Chapter 1, I established my starting point in any discussion about God. "The Bible is what it says it is, and God is who he says He is in the Bible." What does the Bible say that it says it is?

"All scripture is inspired by God and is useful for teaching, for reproof, for correction and for training in righteousness, so that everyone who belongs to God may be proficient, equipped for every good work." (2 Timothy 3:16-17 NRSV)

"All Scripture is God-breathed and is useful for teaching, rebuking, correcting and training in righteousness, so that the servant of God may be thoroughly equipped for every good work." (2 Timothy 3:16-17 NIV)

This is an important starting point. The Holy Bible, a collection of books written by many people over centuries, describes itself as being "inspired by God," or "God-breathed." We may not like the bit about reproof or correction, but keep in mind what you have just read about sin separating us from God and the definition of righteousness in our definitions. The Bible, as God's inspired means of communicating with us, is also relevant to today's needs.

"Indeed, the word of God is living and active, sharper than any two-edged sword, piercing until it divides soul from spirit, joints from marrow; it is able to judge the thoughts and intentions of the heart. And before him no creature is hidden, but all are naked and laid bare to the eyes of the one to whom we must render an account." (Hebrews 4:12-13)

The God of the Bible, Our God, is a living and active God and His Word, the Bible, is living and active. That means that when we read it prayerfully, seeking truth or help in our day-to-day, twenty first century living, we can depend on God speaking to us through His Word about our current circumstances. This is not a "nice" book of quotations; it is not a philosophy book, nor just a history book. It is the revealed, true, living Word of God. It is God speaking to you when you read the text, so as you read the Bible, ask the Lord for the help of His Holy Spirit. Be prepared to be challenged, rebuked or corrected of your living if your lifestyle is not of God. You can also expect that God will minister to you in a relevant way, give you peace and an assurance of His presence, or guide you in your life's journey as you search the scriptures.

It is critical for you to understand that my book is not God's Word, other than when the passages from the Bible are quoted. That said, you can expect God to speak to you through this book as you read it because my comments are made to try to explain the context of when the Word was written and some comments about the events around which the Bible speaks.

Jesus accepted what was effectively the Old Testament as God's Word. He speaks of "The Law and the Prophets", and particularly in Matthew 22:37-40, in response to a question from the Pharisees who tried to put him to the test about which was the greatest commandment in the law, replied, "You shall love the Lord your God with all your heart, and with all your soul, and with all your mind.' This is the greatest and first commandment. And a second is like it: 'You shall love your neighbor as yourself.' On these two commandments hang all the law and the prophets." In the incident of the Rich man and Lazarus (Luke 16:19-31) Abraham, speaking from heaven to the rich man in hell, gave credence to the writings when he said, "If they do not listen to Moses and the Prophets, they will not be convinced, even if someone rises from the dead."

Before touching on the promises God has made, or his covenants, may we look at what a promise or agreement entails. If I gave you an IOU, a cheque or signed an agreement to buy or sell something, there are two sides to the agreement. There is the giver and the receiver. The giver of the IOU has a responsibility or obligation to the receiver to actually come good on the promise, to fulfill the initial agreement. The receiver, on the other hand, has a reasonable expectation that the giver will come good. There is, on the one hand, an obligation and responsibility to fulfill the promise and on the other hand, a reasonable expectation that the promise will be fulfilled.

It is an incredible situation where the Infinite, Eternal God, creator of heaven and earth, should obligate himself to his created by making covenants or agreements with us his creatures. Obligation – Expectation. It is critical to our understanding and our attitude to living that we must remind ourselves that God's covenant, agreement, or promises made with us and to us for our benefit come with an expectation that we also have responsibilities and obligations to fulfill.

In the Old Testament, there are four major covenants recorded – with Noah, Abraham, the Israelites and King David. God obligates himself with the promises made to people, but the promises come with a tag that is directly linked to Godly living and behavior on the Israelite's side of the agreement. There are consequences of breaking the agreement once entered. God's initial desire when he created people was for it "to be good". We were created in his image – not a visual image because God is an invisible spirit, but able to think conceptually, react and love. The whole story of the Bible is of the Creator, through His grace, making a pathway to be reconciled with himself. The prophet Jeremiah captures this in Jeremiah 30:22: "And you shall be my people, and I will be your God."

In the prayer of dedication to the temple in 1Kings 8:23-24, Solomon prayed. "He said, 'O Lord, God of Israel, there is no God like you in heaven above or on earth beneath, keeping covenant and steadfast love for your servants who walk before you with all their heart, the covenant that you kept for your servant my father David as you declared to him; you promised with your mouth and have this day fulfilled with your hand.'"

Very early in the historical records of God's chosen people is where we need to start to look at the effort and energy God has expended to bring humankind back into fellowship with himself. I have mentioned expectation and obligation and it is essential that we recognize there is both an expectation and obligation on both sides of the partnership. In extending his promises or covenants to us, God does put covenants on the covenants. For his obligation to us to ensure he fulfils his promise, God has a (reasonable) expectation that we make a conscious decision and choose to lead a life worthy of this agreement. Likewise, we as recipients of God's grace also need to recognize that as a part of our agreement with God, we need to choose to lead a life that is acceptable to God's standards.

Following on from Noah, we pick up the ancestral line of Abram. (Genesis Chapters 11 and on) This relates to the intricate detail of God's unfolding of His Plan A and the key word in all of this is the word *redemption*. A search of the dictionary definition gives me these meanings -

an act of redeeming or atoning for a fault or mistake, or the state of being redeemed. deliverance; rescue. *Theology*. deliverance from sin; salvation. atonement for guilt. Paying off, as of a mortgage, bond, or note. (IOU?)

Please pause and think on this for a moment, linking what we read in Chapter 1 about God's Plan A.

The Lord Jesus Christ, Son of God yet God, part of the creation Godhead who existed before time began and people were created, knew that Adam and Eve would sin and need to be banished from God's presence. Yet from the beginning, and rather than being caught unawares, God set into place a plan of redemption for us all. God wants to rescue us. He wants to deliver us from sin and its consequences. He wants to provide salvation for Eternity. He wants to create this state of atonement – at "one"ment with Himself. He wants to pay out our mortgage or bond.

The Promises / Covenants

1. To Noah

The first covenant promise made to Noah and through him to the whole human race is that He will never, ever flood the earth again as a form of judgment because of wicked living. And his sign to remind himself of this promise? The rainbow. The rainbow reminds God of his own covenant. It is interesting that this beautiful, natural phenomenon has been hijacked by groups of people who are flouting God's promise back in his face by its use as their symbol. For your own reading, you can pick up the life story of Noah in Genesis Chapters 6 to 9.

"This is like the days of Noah to me: Just as I swore that the waters of Noah would never again go over the earth, so I have sworn that I will not be angry with you and will not rebuke you. For the mountains may depart and the hills be removed, but my steadfast love shall not depart from you, and my covenant of peace shall not be removed, says the Lord, who has compassion on you." (Isaiah 54:9-10)

2. To Abram/Abraham

The Call of Abram

There are two strands to God's covenant with Abraham. It was the multiplication of Abraham's offspring, even before there were any, and the second part of the covenant was the inheritance of The Promised Land – the land of Israel that was reputed to be flowing with milk and honey.

"Now the Lord said to Abram, 'Go from your country and your kindred and your father's house to the land that I will show you. I will make of you a great nation, and I will bless you, and make your name great, so that you will be a blessing. I will bless those who bless you, and the one who curses you I will curse; and in you all the families of the earth shall be blessed.'" (Genesis 12:1-3)

Genesis Chapter 15:6 states: "And he (Abram) believed the Lord, and the Lord reckoned it to him as righteousness."

Later, in a special time with Abram, God changed his name to Abraham, the father of many nations, and the purpose of this covenant was in effect to restore the initial creation relationship. "I will establish my covenant between me and you, and your offspring after you throughout their generations, for an everlasting covenant, to be God to you and to your offspring after you." (Genesis 17:7 – but read around these verses to capture the full incident)

This personal connection with being the exclusive God of the Israelites is captured somewhat when we read the story of Ruth and Naomi in the book of Ruth, when Ruth said to her mother-in-law, Naomi, "Do not press me to leave you or to turn back from following you! Where you go, I will go; where you lodge, I will lodge; your people shall be my people and your God my God." (Ruth 1:16)

At the birth of John the Baptist, his father Zechariah is recorded as singing and prophesying about the culmination of the Old Testament prophecies.

"Then his father Zechariah was filled with the Holy Spirit and spoke this prophecy: 'Blessed be the Lord God of Israel, for he has looked favorably on his people and redeemed them. He has raised up a mighty Saviour for us in the house of his servant David, as he spoke through the mouth of his holy prophets from of old, that we would be saved from our enemies and from the hand of all who hate us. Thus he has shown the mercy promised to our ancestors, and has remembered his holy covenant, the oath that he swore to our ancestor Abraham, to grant us that we, being rescued from the hands of our enemies, might serve him without fear.'" (Luke 1:67-74)

Into this concept of "right living" we are also introducing the concept of faith and belief. This is an integral part of the "fine print" of the covenants established by God with us, his people.

3. To Moses

We step forward four hundred years (Read Genesis 15:13) to the time when the Israelites (Descendants of Jacob who was renamed Israel, descendants of Isaac, son of Abraham and Sarah) when God heard the prayers of these enslaved people – his chosen people. To get the full background, maybe it would be good to pause for a moment and read Exodus Chapters 1 through to 6. Make a note of the number of times you read the words "concerned", "rescue", or "deliverance".

The Exodus saga shows a time of obedience and disobedience, of faith and absolute lack of faith and trust in God and his promises. It is a time that God used to teach the Israelite people the need to have faith in His promises – to be a faithful people and to be a people full of faith.

As you read the passage of the Exodus and the events recorded, these incidents do not need to be repeated for every generation because they were recorded then, and we can glean from the lessons learned how we need to react to similar circumstances. It was during these wanderings that God started to forge people of character and dependence on Him and they were prepared to enter the Promised Land little by little. I will touch on some of the Old Testament heroes of faith later.

The Exodus was effectively the starting point and the main reference point historically for God's chosen people. Devout Jewish people would be well versed in the Exodus because it was a constant reminder to them as they read The Torah.

In Exodus 6:1, we read, "Then the Lord said to Moses, 'Now you shall see what I will do to Pharoah: Indeed by a mighty hand he will let them go; by a mighty hand he will drive them out of his land.'" After the amazing series of events that led to their final release, we read in Exodus 14:31, "Israel saw the great work that the Lord did against the Egyptians. So the people feared the Lord and believed in the Lord and in his servant Moses."

This event, the deliverance from 430 years of slavery, was a pivotal, historical point in the history of God's chosen people, the descendants of Abraham. So much so that it was constantly referred to as the turning point in their history. When God issued the Ten Commandments on Mount Sinai very early in the Exodus escape, God prefixed the Commandments with these words: "I am the Lord your God, who brought you out of the land of Egypt, out of the house of slavery." (Exodus 20:2)

Ezekiel 16:60-62 records, "Yet I will remember my covenant with you in the days of your youth, and I will establish with you an everlasting covenant. … I will establish my covenant with you, and you shall know that I am the Lord."

Deuteronomy 5 1-11 relates the initiation of the Ten Commandments. (Read through to verse 33 to capture the full incident.) "Moses convened all Israel, and said to them: 'Hear, O Israel, the statutes and ordinances that I am addressing to you today; you shall learn them and observe them diligently. The Lord our God made a covenant with us at Horeb. Not with our ancestors did the Lord make this covenant, but with us, who are all of us here alive today. The Lord spoke with you face to face at the mountain, out of the fire. (At that time I was standing between the Lord and you to declare to you the words of the Lord; for you were afraid because of the fire and did not go up the mountain.) And he said: 'I am the Lord your God, who brought you out of the land of Egypt, out of the house of slavery; you shall have no other gods before me. You shall not make for yourself an idol, whether in the form of anything that is in heaven above or that is on the earth beneath, or that is in the water under the earth. You shall not bow down to them or worship them; for I the Lord your God am a jealous God, punishing children for the iniquity of parents, to the third and fourth generation of those who reject me, but showing steadfast love to the thousandth generation of those who love me and keep my commandments. You shall not make wrongful use of the name of the Lord your God, for the Lord will not acquit anyone who misuses his name.'"

These words were to echo throughout their history – Deuteronomy 5:6/13:10, Joshua 24:17, Judges 6:8, Jeremiah 34:13, Micah 6:4.

An Aside – When the covenant is broken

It is important to pause for a moment to consider what were the penalties imposed by God for when any of the covenants were broken. There has never been a time, and never will be, when God broke His side of the covenant, but what happened when his people broke the covenant?

In anticipation of this situation, God instituted a very detailed and complex system of sacrifices to be made and strict conditions imposed on their procedures. This should not come as any surprise, for when we look at the attention to detail in creation, and the intricate way all of creation is woven together, we should be recognizing that God is the God of minute detail and attention to detail. God is also a Holy God, so this willful breaking of his covenant (which, remember, is called sin) means that he cannot abide this sinfulness and needs to turn away until the sin is atoned.

There were many sacrifices instituted by the Lord, including celebratory feasts recognizing his involvement in the rescue of the chosen race of people. The Passover is probably the most recognizable reason for celebration and it was a constant reminder that God rescued people from 430 years of slavery.

The mobile Tent of Meeting used by the people of the Exodus was detailed in its construction, with a reason and a purpose for every aspect of the meeting point, and the process of sacrifices to be made at various times of the season. The shedding of blood was a symbolic action representing the giving of life, so the symbolic process undertaken by a devout Jewish person was to touch the animal being slaughtered, making the connection with that animal's life being substituted for the person's life.

In short, I think we can summarise this situation of being reconciled to God by the need to believe that God exists, that the promises God made can be accepted with reliability, that God is a Holy God and that the sinfulness of the chosen people (and us) needs to be cleansed and forgiven. So, the looking forward to a Messiah for deliverance was something anticipated, but in many ways, in the eyes of the Jews, there was little connection between the rescue of Jesus from our slavery to sin and the lessons from the Old Testament's 2000 years of history.

Sacrifices

Throughout the Old Testament records, we find there are numerous forms of sacrifice ordained by God for different purposes. Sacrificial offering was something in common practice in other nations of antiquity so it wasn't exclusive to the worship of Yahweh alone. There were fire offerings of sacrifice, burnt offerings, where the sacrificial animal was eaten by the priests, or by the people together. There was cereal offering for the celebration of the first fruits of the season, and there was provision made for poor people to be able to offer a less expensive offering, such as a pair of doves instead of a lamb. Sacrificial offerings, often accompanied by celebratory feasts, were for dedications, new beginnings, thanksgiving for abundance, or deliverance such as the main celebration – The Passover.

The Passover was an annual reminder that God led the Israelite people from slavery in Egypt with the passing over of the angel of death over the Egyptian people because of their faith in sacrificing a lamb, and placing the blood on the lintel of their homes. The narrative of this event to be remembered can be found in Exodus 12 that followed the plagues that were used to catch Pharoah's attention and soften his heart.

So important was this historical and pivotal event that when God issued the Ten Commandments, the prefix to them relate to the following words: "Then God spoke all these words: 'I am the Lord your God, who brought you out of the land of Egypt, out of the house of slavery.'" (Exodus 20:1)

We will come to the New Testament readings that show us that Christ became the Passover Lamb that was sacrificed. "Clean out the old yeast so that you may be a new batch, as you really are unleavened. For our paschal lamb, Christ, has been sacrificed." (1 Corinthians 5:7) This is why it is important to understand that Jesus' crucifixion was during the Feast of the Passover in Jerusalem. Hebrews Chapter 9 links this very clearly: "But when Christ came as a high priest of the good things that have come, then through the greater and perfect tent (not made with hands, that is, not of this creation), he entered once for all into the Holy

Place, not with the blood of goats and calves, but with his own blood, thus obtaining eternal redemption." (Hebrews 9:11-12)

To stress on the people his holiness, there were very strict and specific rules given as to how the sacrifice was to be prepared and offered. The motivation was the honouring of God, thanksgiving for his goodness, and more solemnly as a means of restoring the fellowship with him by seeking his forgiveness for sin through the shedding of blood of the sacrificial lamb, and by identifying with the sacrifice by placing one's hand on the beast.

In response to King Saul's claim that he had done as requested in the slaying of the Amalekites, but had brought some of the animals back to camp to offer as burnt offerings, Samuel replied: "Has the Lord as great delight in burnt offerings and sacrifices, as in obedience to the voice of the Lord? Surely, to obey is better than sacrifice and to heed than the fat of rams. For rebellion is no less a sin than divination, and stubbornness is like iniquity and idolatry. Because you have rejected the word of the Lord, he has also rejected you from being king."(1 Samuel 15:22-23)

This personal application to the concept of sacrifice as a means of atonement is all the more personalized in other verses in the Bible. Psalm 51:17 reads, "The sacrifice acceptable to God is a broken spirit; a broken and contrite heart, O God, you will not despise." Matthew 9:13 states, "Go and learn what this means, 'I desire mercy, not sacrifice.' For I have come to call not the righteous but sinners." While Romans 12:1 reads, "I appeal to you therefore, brothers and sisters, by the mercies of God, to present your bodies as a living sacrifice, holy and acceptable to God, which is your spiritual worship."

4. To King David

In similar terms to the earlier covenants we have briefly examined, the Davidic covenant was also mostly promissory. With the changes in governance, and the consecration of David as King, the main mediator between God and His people, a new covenant became necessary. The main thrust of this covenant was the eternal reign by his descendants. If you read 2 Samuel 7, this outlines God's prophecy to King David through the prophet Samuel and it leads to the birth of Jesus through David's line of descendants. We pick up affirmations of God's covenant with David in the following verses.

"Incline your ear, and come to me; listen, so that you may live. I will make with you an everlasting covenant, my steadfast, sure love for David." (Isaiah 55:3)

"And I the Lord, **will be their God, and my servant David** shall be prince among them; **I the** Lord **have spoken."** (Ezekiel 34:24)

As well as the covenants or binding agreements that God entered into with these four important people, the Old Testament is full of prophecies pointing to the coming to Earth of Jesus as the chosen Messiah, even if this term is not used. It is important as you read this section and read of the foretelling of the coming of Jesus that these verses are taken from the Old Testament as we now call it. To the Jewish people it is taken from The Law and the Prophets, the very collection of writing to that which Jesus gave his affirmation, as we have already discussed.

The greater part of the Old Testament after the Psalms and Proverbs centres on the Prophets and their roles in God's dealings with the Israelites. The New Testament book of Hebrews begins with the words: "Long ago God spoke to our ancestors in many and various ways by the prophets." (Hebrews 1:1) So what was the message of these special people selected by God?

David to Jesus – The Prophecies

Jesus Christ – Son of God - Saviour

You will need to bear with me in this short time because I will be jumping from the Old Testament to statements made by Jesus as recorded in the New Testament.

Following from the last paragraph above, where I quoted Hebrews 1:1, this verse goes on to record in verse 2, "But in these last days he has spoken to us by a Son, whom he appointed heir of all things, through whom he also created the worlds."

The Christian faith is, by its name, a faith based on Christ. The Old Testament writings and the key message of the prophets all point to the coming of Jesus to live on Earth. Paul writes in 2 Corinthians 1:20, "For no matter how many promises God has made, they are 'Yes' in Christ."(NIV)

From King David through to Jesus' incarnation, we face a time span of around 1000 years and that stemming from the call of Abram close to another 1000 years. Effectively there are two parallel streams to follow. The most important stream is the human genealogy that can be accurately traced that led to Jesus' birth. The second stream is to follow the historical account of the growing group of people into what was to become the Nation of Israel. This follows the conquest of the Jewish people by surrounding Kingdoms and Exile into foreign lands such as Babylon. Intertwined with these historical accounts we find prophets emerging to either warn the people of God's judgment because of their willful disobedience, coupled with the prophesying of the coming of a Messiah or Redeemer.

For us reading these texts and studying the Bible and its prophecies, it is very easy to see the pattern of prophecy and their fulfillment. But to the Jewish people living in the 1000 years between Abraham and the coming of Jesus, while there would have been a sense of expectation of a deliverer for their nation, the clues given in the Law and the Prophets and Psalms are all very cryptic and not that easy to understand. You have probably learned that the Old Testament points to Jesus, whereas the New Testament is about Jesus, but nowhere in the writings of the Old Testament do we read terms such as "Messiah", "Jesus" or "Jesus Christ". Instead there are terms used such as messenger as we read in Malachi, the last book of the Old Testament, written some 450 years before Jesus and he wrote, "See, I am sending my messenger to prepare the way before me, and the Lord whom you seek will suddenly come to his temple. The messenger of the covenant in whom you delight—indeed, he is coming, says the Lord of hosts." (Malachi 3:1).

Various prophets were raised by God throughout Israel's history as a means of communicating with the people to warn them, chastise them, or encourage them, but all with the same aim: to restore the relationship of the people chosen by God with Himself. Some of the prophets had to warn of forthcoming military incursions or weather calamities. Others looked to the coming of a Messiah, to the coming of Jesus, and this was often part of a mixed message foretold and forth told.

Isaiah the prophet, for example, spends a great deal of the prophecy as recorded in the book of the same name speaking of the judgment of Jerusalem and Judah, along with planned judgments on Assyria, Babylon, the Philistines and Moab and other regions and kingdoms. There is a distinct turn to the prophecy towards comfort for God's people (Isaiah 40), the Helper of Israel (Ch 41) Israel's only Saviour (Ch 43) through to the Restoration of Israel and Everlasting Salvation for Zion. (Ch 51)

Read the following passage, but please spend some time thinking on it, both from a historical perspective of something written about 700 years before Jesus, and also from the perspective of the disciples during their time with Jesus. Compare this lack of knowledge with the knowledge of what has happened as we read this passage today.

Isaiah 53:1-8: "Who has believed what we have heard? And to whom has the arm of the Lord been revealed? For he grew up before him like a young plant, and like a root out of dry ground; he had no form or majesty that we should look at him, nothing in his appearance that we should desire him. He was despised and rejected by others; a man of suffering and acquainted with infirmity; and as one from whom others hide their faces he was despised, and we held him of no account.

Surely he has borne our infirmities and carried our diseases; yet we accounted him stricken, struck down by God, and afflicted. But he was wounded for our transgressions, crushed for our iniquities; upon him was the punishment that made us whole, and by his bruises we are healed. All we like sheep have gone astray; we have all turned to our own way, and the Lord has laid on him the iniquity of us all.

"He was oppressed, and he was afflicted, yet he did not open his mouth; like a lamb that is led to the slaughter, and like a sheep that before its shearers is silent, so he did not open his mouth. By a perversion of justice he was taken away. Who could have imagined his future? For he was cut off from the land of the living, stricken for the transgression of my people."

This book was written around 700 years before Jesus and it was this section of Isaiah the Ethiopian eunuch was reading while sitting on his chariot returning to Ethiopia after worshipping in Jerusalem. Phillip, led by the Holy Spirit, caught up to him when "The eunuch asked Philip, 'About whom, may I ask you, does the prophet say this, about himself or about someone else?' Then Philip began to speak, and starting with this scripture, he proclaimed to him the good news about Jesus."

It is good to read this narrative in Acts 8:26-40 because it demonstrates the reality of God's word being "living and active". Phillip met the high-ranking official from Ethiopia and it was no accident that he was reading the scroll about Isaiah's prophecy of Jesus' role. While you are reading this book, or the Bible passages, there may be something stirring within you that you sense is God's Spirit touching your life. Be open to this prompting.

A prophecy in Zechariah 13:7 states, "Awake, O sword, against my shepherd, against the man who is my associate," says the Lord of hosts. "Strike the shepherd, that the sheep may be scattered; I will turn my hand against the little ones."

Jesus quoted this prophecy when he predicted Peter's denial, and we read it quoted in Matthew 26:31: "Then Jesus said to them, 'You will all become deserters because of me this night; for it is written, 'I will strike the shepherd, and the sheep of the flock will be scattered.'"

During his very short time of three years of ministry, Jesus referred to some Old Testament writings and some writings about himself, which now we can see as the results of the puzzle. Scholars and Rabbis in discussion would have promulgated their personal theories about what some of the passages meant, but there were probably more questions asked than answered. As Jesus began his ministry in the synagogue in Nazareth, he read from the following verses of Isaiah 61:1-2.

The Good News of Deliverance

"The spirit of the Lord God is upon me, because the Lord has anointed me; he has sent me to bring good news to the oppressed, to bind up the brokenhearted, to proclaim liberty to the captives, and release to the prisoners; to proclaim the year of the Lord's favour, and the day of vengeance of our God; to comfort all who mourn."

Luke captures the scene in Luke 4:20-21: **"And he rolled up the scroll, gave it back to the attendant, and sat down. The eyes of all in the synagogue were fixed on him. Then he began to say to them, "Today this scripture has been fulfilled in your hearing."**

Understand if you can, the impact Jesus' statement about the fulfillment of a well-known prophecy in Himself. We have the hindsight of history. The Jewish leaders would have been astonished that this carpenter's son would even dare to claim the fulfillment of the prophecy.

Deuteronomy 18 (selected verses) speaks of a prophet who would be raised up from among the Jewish nation:

"The Lord your God will raise up for you a prophet like me from among your own people; you shall heed such a prophet.... Then the Lord replied to me "They are right in what they have said. I will raise up for them a prophet like you from among their own people; I will put my words in the mouth of the prophet, who shall speak to them everything that I command. ... You may say to yourself, "How can we recognize a word that the Lord has not spoken?" If a prophet speaks in the name of the Lord but the thing does not take place or prove true, it is a word that the Lord has not spoken. The prophet has spoken it presumptuously; do not be frightened by it."

The New Testament cites OT Scripture to support the claim of early Christians that Jesus was the promised Messiah and from there to affirm that He would return to Earth at some time in the future. Most of the prophetic references are taken from the Book of Isaiah, but sadly, Jewish people today do not regard any of these prophecies as having been fulfilled by Jesus or have any Messianic references at all.

Matthew's gospel presents Jesus' ministry as fulfillment of the prophecies made in Isaiah, but I need to emphasise to you that this Gospel was written after Jesus' ascension, so the disciples did not have any historical references to draw upon in their final days with Jesus. These prophecies would have been well known to Jewish people of Jesus' time – to his disciples. They would have been read in synagogues and discussed at length, but to the disciples accompanying Jesus during his three years of ministry, to start to try to get a handle on it all – to seeing the prophecies being fulfilled - would have been met with an air of disbelief more than a lack of faith.

The Genealogy of Jesus

The genealogy of Jesus is listed (slightly differently) in both Matthew and Luke and it is listed to show how Jesus was a person of human descent. Starting with the accurate recording of the people in each of the twelve tribes of Israel, named because of the leadership of the twelve sons of Jacob (Israel), the line of descendancy to Jesus can be followed easily. It is not my intention to detail this, but you can follow the line in Matthew Chapter 1:1-17 and Luke 3:23-38. I found it interesting to trace each of the names listed and find them in the Old Testament using a Google search or a Bible Concordance. You may be interested to do the same, but be prepared for some "cultural" shocks.

Heroes of the Old Testament

The history of humankind described throughout the Old Testament with studies in varying degrees of intimacy of the people mentioned throughout the two thousand years of history reveals a diverse range of characters. While the society would be described as a Patriarchal Society, not all of the "heroes" of the Old Testament were men. There are incidents recorded of achievements and failures of men, women and children, some whose names are recorded and many who are mentioned, but we don't know their name.

In the New Testament, Chapter 11 of the book of Hebrews could be named the Hebrews Hall of Faith Fame. It is bookended by two sets of verses about faith – verses 1 and 39.

"Now faith is the assurance of things hoped for, the conviction of things not seen. Indeed, by faith our ancestors received approval."

"Yet all these, though they were commended for their faith, did not receive what was promised, since God had provided something better so that they would not, apart from us, be made perfect."

Living today, we have ready access to the Bible and numerous books written on every subject that is useful for us to read. Spare a thought for the early people mentioned in Hebrews – Abel, Enoch, Noah and Abram/Abraham. Living in a culture that had some form of religion, these people's lives are recorded as linking with God in various ways, and in obeying God in His direction to their lives. Can you start to understand how Abraham "believed the Lord, and the Lord reckoned it to him as righteousness?"

As a bit of fun, I looked through Hebrews 11 and using a Concordance (nowadays use Google) traced the history narratives of all of the people mentioned in this chapter. You learn of their strengths and weaknesses, but you also learn of their faith.

If the theme of the Old Testament is, "And you shall be my people, and I will be your God", the overarching theme of the Bible is found in Jesus' words in John 20:29: "Have you believed because you have seen me? Blessed are those who have not seen and yet have come to believe." Our faith in God is precious to Almighty God, and in many ways, it is a reflection of how much faith we have is found in how we relate to these truths in his Word.

We are called to be faithful people, and we are encouraged to be full of faith.

The History of the Nation

There is no way I can satisfactorily outline the history of the Israelite nation over the two thousand years of its recorded history from Abraham to Jesus, nor is it the scope of this book to do so. I believe I can briefly summarise the history. Israel prospered when they were faithful and obedient to the Lord. In times of disobedience and faithlessness, God, whose sole aim, remember, is to redeem and reclaim them for fellowship with himself, caught their attention either through natural calamities such as severe drought or crop failure, or dispossession of their land through exile, or being taken over by a foreign power.

As The Lord appeared to Solomon after the temple building had been completed, these verses summarise God's relationship with His people well.

"I have heard your prayer and have chosen this place for myself as a temple for sacrifices. When I shut up the heavens so that there is no rain, or command locusts to devour the land or send a plague among my people, if my people, who are called by my name, will humble themselves and pray and seek my face and turn from their wicked ways, then I will hear from heaven, and I will forgive their sin and will heal their land." (2 Chronicles 7:12-14)

Never before has this concept been more relevant than today. World wide, legislation is being enacted that is totally contrary to God's teachings and contrary to His desire for our right living. People's lifestyles are leading totally away from any form of spiritual dimension, or if a dimension that involves a spiritual understanding, it is foreign to the teachings found in the Bible.

Nowhere in the media do we read or hear of people being encouraged to repent and be baptized. Nowhere do we read of people being encouraged to humble themselves and pray and seek God's face. Nowhere are people encouraged to turn from their wicked ways. In fact, in some countries that had a Christian heritage, preaching is against the law and speaking the truth about the sinful ways of life could land the speaker in a prison cell. Hear me clearly here – but the emphasis on the change of the planet through the climate change debate does not claim any of God's principle that with repentance He can heal our land.

I venture to suggest that we need to address two separate issues here that may or may not be connected. People everywhere need to repent and turn back to God, confessing that we have neglected the First Commandment. This repentance needs to be "non-commercial", with no strings attached.

The second issue is for the restoration of our society that includes viable and successful agriculture and manufacturing, economic policies and the like. Both of these issues are beyond the scope of this small book, but they are important issues that need prayerful debate and action from individuals through community to nations. God is a God who has made promises. He has instituted covenants with his created people. The flip side of the agreement is for righteous and holy living, nothing less. God's promises are for community.

"Blessed be the God and Father of our Lord Jesus Christ, the Father of mercies and the God of all consolation, who consoles us in all our affliction, so that we may be able to console those who are in any affliction with the consolation with which we ourselves are consoled by God."(2 Corinthians 1:3-4)

As you read this book, please try to read for your own personal faith walk. As you walk, you will find yourself wanting to be a part of a vibrant Christian community of believers who are also wanting to walk where and how Jesus walked for the benefit of those around you.

God's one desire? "So you will be my people, and I will be your God." (Jeremiah 30:22)

CHAPTER 3

EMMANUEL – GOD WITH US

For most people, the birth of a baby is celebrated with joy and wonder. Pregnancy and the development of a new person "fearfully and wonderfully made ... woven together in the depths of the earth ... made in the secret place" (Psalm 139 – read it all) is one of those beautiful things and part of God's creative abilities exhibited by all living things.

Throughout Christendom, Christmas, the celebration of the birth of the baby Jesus is one of those events that goes almost to an extreme amongst people, including those who have no real belief in God or His purposes, or who want to eliminate the mention of Christ from Christmas.

In the very early days of the exodus from Egypt, God instructed the people and gifted artisans to manufacture a very elaborate and beautiful box (the Ark of the Covenant) that held the stones of the Ten Commandments, and together with the detailed instructions of its construction, had the people make the Tent of Meeting. Because God is an invisible spirit with a nature but no form or substance, He is very strict on the manufacture of images or idols because they restrict him in time and space. However, knowing that we as people being physical (five senses) need to have something tangible to understand the presence of this "something", The Ark of the Covenant and the Tent of Meeting were portable reminders that God was with the Israelites during their sojourn in the desert.

In Chapter 2, Promises and Prophecies, we briefly looked at parts of the writings of the Old Testament that pointed to the coming of a Redeemer or Messiah, whose purpose (God's Plan A) was to pave the way back to God for those who believe. There are two parts to this next part of God's history and they are integral to the other.

Emmanuel means God with us. Christmas is a celebration of the birth of this unique person – Jesus Christ, Son of God, Saviour.

The coming of Jesus in the form of a person – 100% human, 100% God – really had a two-fold purpose. It is this purpose, God's purpose that we will examine in this chapter.

The purposes behind Jesus' Advent

1. For Eternal Salvation – God's Plan A

In essence, this short section of the book in Chapter 1 outlined the Good News of the Gospel of the Lord Jesus Christ. There was also the devotion "Why bother"? This ended with the conclusion that God's motivation is love.

The Almighty, Infinite, Eternal, Omnipotent, Omniscient, Omnipresent, Never changing and Everlasting God who cannot be contained, who spoke and the whole of creation came into being and saw that it was good, has an infinite love for His creation that knows no bounds. A love that is intimate and personal and is exhibited in the love shown in the coming of His Son, Jesus Christ, to live on Earth away from Heaven for a period of thirty three years. It is a love that history records drew him to the crucifixion in a barbaric, cruel and painful way, and it is a love that saw him enter hell, a complete separation from God the Father for the first time ever in Eternity.

Let me share just some of the Bible statements that refer to this love of Jesus. In the opening pages of this book, I said the Bible was a love letter from God. I also wrote what I believe is a good summary of the Bible in one sentence. God speaking says, "John, (insert your name) I love you because I made you, I want to spend Eternity with you and I want your life to reflect this." It should therefore come as no surprise to find numerous references to God's love and the affirmations of his love.

These words echo throughout human history, but they are more than historical statements. They affirm that GOD LOVES YOU! Whenever you read the word "you", the Bible is meaning you – the reader. Wherever you are, whatever your situation, whatever your past life, God loves you. God loves you the person. There are many references here from God's living and active word. As you read, maybe some of the verses resonate within your heart and life. Do not be surprised about this. It is God's Holy Spirit ministering to you and to your life. Listen to them – respond to their promptings. As Jesus said, "Let anyone with ears listen!"

Jeremiah 31:3

"The Lord appeared to him from far away. I have loved you with an everlasting love; therefore I have continued my faithfulness to you."

John 3:16

"For God so loved the world that he gave his only Son, that everyone who believes in him may not perish but have eternal life."

John 15:13

"No one has greater love has no one than this, to lay down one's life for one's friends."

Romans 5:7-8

"Indeed, rarely will anyone die for a righteous person—though perhaps for a good person someone might actually dare to die. But God proves his love for us in that while we still were sinners Christ died for us."

1 John 4:8-16

"Whoever does not love does not know God, for God is love. God's love was revealed among us in this way: God sent his only Son into the world so that we might live through him. In this is love, not that we loved God but that he loved us and sent his Son to be the atoning sacrifice for our sins. Beloved, since God loved us so much, we also ought to love one another. No one has ever seen God; if we love one another, God lives in us, and his love is perfected in us.

"By this we know that we abide in him and he in us, because he has given us of his Spirit. And we have seen and do testify that the Father has sent his Son as the Savior of the world. God abides in those who confess that Jesus is the Son of God, and they abide in God. So we have known and believe the love that God has for us.

"God is love, and those who abide in love abide in God, and God abides in them." Ephesians 3:14-21

Prayer for the Readers

"For this reason I bow my knees before the Father, from whom every family in heaven and on earth takes its name. I pray that, according to the riches of his glory, he may grant that you may be strengthened in your inner being with power through his Spirit, and that Christ may dwell in your hearts through faith, as you are being rooted and grounded in love. I pray that you may have the power to comprehend, with all the saints, what is the breadth and length and height and depth, and to know the love of Christ that surpasses knowledge, so that you may be filled with all the fullness of God.

"Now to him who by the power at work within us is able to accomplish abundantly far more than all we can ask or imagine, to him be glory in the church and in Christ Jesus to all generations, forever and ever. Amen." Romans 8:31-39

God's Love in Christ Jesus

"What then are we to say about these things? If God is for us, who is against us? He who did not withhold his own Son, but gave him up for all of us, will he not with him also give us everything else? Who will bring any charge against God's elect? It is God who justifies. Who is to condemn? It is Christ Jesus, who died, yes, who was raised, who is at the right hand of God, who indeed intercedes for us. Who will separate us from the love of Christ? Will hardship, or distress, or persecution, or famine, or nakedness, or peril, or sword? As it is written,

"For your sake we are being killed all day long; we are accounted as sheep to be slaughtered."

"No, in all these things we are more than conquerors through him who loved us. For I am convinced that neither death, nor life, nor angels, nor rulers, nor things present, nor things to come, nor powers, nor height, nor depth, nor anything else in all creation, will be able to separate us from the love of God in Christ Jesus our Lord."

There is a balance and a connection and that is the grace of God. The grace of God is defined as "unmerited favour". We do not deserve any of what God offers, and in fact, the whole of God's Plan A is one of God's grace to us, the created. In the section about the Old Testament, there was a heavy emphasis on the need for sacrifices to atone for our sin. Many think the Ten Commandments are a list of things given from a "spoil-sport" God, and this may appear to be the case, until you start to fully understand the full picture presented in the Bible. Refer back to the definitions I presented where you have a choice – one thing or another. Love God or reject God. I refer to the First Commandment a few times throughout our journey because it is this First Commandment that is the integral part of our ongoing relationship with God. We must honour Him as God, Lord and Master.

The second part of the next quotation from Deuteronomy assures me there are two sides to the one story and I have highlighted these two sides.

Deuteronomy 5:8-10

"You shall not make for yourself an idol, whether in the form of anything that is in heaven above, or that is on the earth beneath, or that is in the water under the earth. You shall not bow down to them or worship them; for I the Lord your God am a jealous God, punishing children for the iniquity of parents, to the third and fourth generation of those who reject me, but showing steadfast love to the thousandth generation of those who love me and keep my commandments."

The grace of God is that free gift of unmerited favour that only comes from God, the Creator of all. I am a Christian because of a number of factors, many unknown to me. People have prayed for me in my past. God's spirit has spoken to my heart, and over a period of time I have responded. I have responded because God's Holy Spirit has softened my heart to the things of God. Daily, I am thankful to the Lord for his grace extended to me and to my family. It is the acceptance of this grace and my thankfulness to the Lord for this grace that encourages me to keep the faith, teach his Word to others and serve Him to the best of my ability with perseverance.

If you sense the presence of God's grace in your life, then be thankful. If you don't have that sense of his grace and feel that you need to feel the touch of his hand, then continue to read this book. Make it your prayer that the Lord will soften your heart to the things of God and extend his grace to you for your life. It is my prayer as I write, knowing that there will come a time when some will read this, that you are touched by the Spirit of God and that you unfold the wonderful, personal application of God's Plan A for your life.

As a living example of both God and Mankind.

It is essential that any study of the Bible must be a study that relates to the reader as a person, with the aim of understanding how God treats us as unique individuals. Being created by God "in His image" puts us on a plane far above the Animal Kingdom, of which biologically we are members. But being created in the image of God enables us to think conceptually (and not just instinctively) and also gives us an ability to have those beautiful emotions such as love. Created with a soul or spirit (and that is so hard to define) also enables us to communicate with our Creator. Being able to think also gives us a freedom of choice in our decision-making, so while we are created by God, we have the ability to make a choice, a free choice insofar as how we relate to God.

In our discussion about eternal salvation, the emphasis was on being made right with God – righteousness. From the moment we surrender our hearts and lives to Jesus to make that conscious decision to freely choose to be one with God, a process called Sanctification begins. This is often called "saint if i cation", or the process of making us like a new creature. God is interested in our character development and the growth process we go through to become less of a sinner and more of a saint. And let me assure you, this is a lifelong process.

Christian bookshops are filled with books that are a great help to us in this process, but I want to share just two sets of verses with you. The first comes from the book of Romans Chapter 8 just before the reading above on love.

Romans 8:28-29

"We know that all things work together for good for those who love God, who are called according to his purpose. For those whom he foreknew he also predestined to be *conformed to the image of his Son*, in order that he might be the firstborn within a large family." (*italics mine*)

Based on the understanding that God is Omnipotent, Omniscient and Omnipresent (powerful, knowing and everywhere), heartened by Jesus' words, "Are not two sparrows sold for a penny? Yet not one of them will fall to the ground apart from your Father." (Matthew 10:29) We need to investigate just what is God's purpose.

What was God's initial purpose in creating you and me? To enjoy fellowship with him all of our days. What of God's eternal purpose to be achieved by Jesus living and dying on a voluntary basis as the sacrifice for our sin? To be a part of the resurrection and to live with God for eternity. God's purpose for you and me while living on earth? Read through to verse 29: *"to be conformed to the image of his Son."*

God's abiding purpose? To become more like Jesus. Yet the strengthening fact is we are not left alone, while the conundrum is we have the choice to go it alone. Notice from the verses from Romans 8:28-29 above, these verses are followed by that beautiful passage from Romans 8 verses 31 onward.

God's Love in Christ Jesus

"What then are we to say about these things? If God is for us, who is against us? He who did not withhold his own Son, but gave him up for all of us, will he not with him also give us everything else? Who will bring any charge against God's elect? It is God who justifies. Who is to condemn? It is Christ Jesus, who died, yes, who was raised, who is at the right hand of God, who indeed intercedes for us. Who will separate us from the love of Christ? Will hardship, or distress, or persecution, or famine, or nakedness, or peril, or sword? As it is written,

"For your sake we are being killed all day long; we are accounted as sheep to be slaughtered."

"No, in all these things we are more than conquerors through him who loved us. "For I am convinced that neither death, nor life, nor angels, nor rulers, nor things present, nor things to come, nor powers, nor height, nor depth, nor anything else in all creation, will be able to separate us from the love of God in Christ Jesus our Lord."

The second part of the benefit of Jesus living on earth as a 100% human is to show us, by perfect example, how to lead and live a godly life. How to love our neighbor or our enemy; how to trust in God; how to have a life that is full of faith; how to be a faithful Christian person; how to spend each day in daily communication with our eternal Creator.

Please come back with me 400 years before Jesus lived on earth to the last recorded prophetic words in the book of Malachi – the last book of the Old Testament. Malachi was writing prophetically concerning the coming of Jesus, and when you consider earthly time, it was a long time coming, with no extra prophetic statements after his time.

Malachi 3:1-3

"See, I am sending my messenger to prepare the way before me, and the Lord whom you seek will suddenly come to his temple. The messenger of the covenant in whom you delight—indeed, he is coming, says the Lord of hosts. But who can endure the day of his coming, and who can stand when he appears?

"For he is like a refiner's fire and like fullers' soap; he will sit as a refiner and purifier of silver, and he will purify the descendants of Levi and refine them like gold and silver, until they present offerings to the Lord in righteousness."

I want to explain a little about verse 3 "**He will sit as a refiner and purifier of silver.**"

This verse is referring to Jesus, but the imagery is of a silversmith processing the silver ore. The rock containing the silver would need to be super heated in a crucible using charcoal and a bellows so that the dross would be burnt off from the molten mixture. The silversmith knew when his silver was pure when he could see his face reflected in the crucible.

Jesus, while still giving you and me the absolute and total freedom to choose how we live, is to be pictured sitting over our life, supervising the burning of the dross so that eventually he can see his face reflected in our life. This concept is captured in James 1:2-4 and 1 Peter 1:7

Trials and Temptations
James 1:2-4

"My brothers and sisters, whenever you face trials of any kind, consider it nothing but joy, because you know that the testing of your faith produces endurance; and let endurance have its full effect, so that you may be mature and complete, lacking in nothing."

1 Peter 1:7

"So that the genuineness of your faith—being more precious than gold that, though perishable, is tested by fire—may be found to result in praise and glory and honor when Jesus Christ is revealed."

So, a very quick but succinct summary: Why did Jesus come to live as a person and what is his example? Where does it lead? We can look to Jesus, the pioneer and perfector of faith. (Hebrews 12:2) We can emulate his life and way of living. We can follow his example in resisting temptation, "Because he himself was tested by what he suffered, he is able to help those who are being tested." (Hebrews 2:18)

Let me say that living like Jesus in a fallen and sinful world, surrounded by people who do not love God, is not an easy task. It wasn't easy for Jesus, as we will see shortly, nor is it easy today. That is why God clearly advises us in His Word the need of being aware.

In 1 John 2:15, a verse On Not Loving the World states, "Do not love the world or the things in the world. The love of the Father is not in those who love the world."

We read in Colossians 3:12-14: "As God's chosen ones, holy and beloved, clothe yourselves with compassion, kindness, humility, meekness, and patience. Bear with one another and, if anyone has a complaint against another, forgive each other; just as the Lord has forgiven you, so you also must forgive. Above all, clothe yourselves with love, which binds everything together in perfect harmony."

Allow me to summarise what it means to have Jesus come among us (then and now):

- The long term Plan A of God is for our redemption. In our reading we have yet to come onto the very important but essential path that Jesus trod while living on Earth for that short period of time, but it is the essence of God's Plan A – redemption of humankind.

- Our salvation is the pathway to be able to spend eternity with God and this is only available through Jesus Christ.

- You and I have the total freedom to choose and accept these facts by faith, or you can choose to reject them. Please be aware of the consequences of rejection of Jesus.

- If you choose to invite Jesus Christ into your life to restore the original intended relationship with your Creator, God is interested in the moulding of your character. Salvation is not just for eternity, but it is for the every day circumstances of living today.

- Your faith is precious to God, as we read in the section about the Old Testament and it has been repeated in the Bible readings above.

- You are saved to serve the Lord, to be a witness to him and his love.

Let us leave this strand for a short time and we will come back to an extension of these thoughts in Chapter 8 "The Rest of Time."

CHAPTER 4

THE "LOST YEARS"

Christmas is over – the long awaited and for some, anticipated birth of Jesus has occurred. And then?

Silence. We have a very sketchy outline of the early years Jesus spent living on earth, so let's look at what we do know. Each of the Gospels tell us something in a different way which helps us to put it together.

The Genealogy of Jesus.

I suggest that you read the opening verses of Matthew 1 from verses 1 to 17 and maybe make a few notes because it does help to understand that none of what we are discussing is random, but really the detailed and attention to detail shown in God's Plan A. To follow through the genealogy at this stage would be a tangent to our discussions, but I do want to suggest you follow through the list of Jesus' ancestors and read of their role in the records of the Bible.

Of particular note is the recording of four ladies' names in a generally male dominated record. Verse 3 – Perez/Tamar (Genesis 38:1-30); verse 5 Boaz the father of Obed, whose mother was Ruth; (Ruth

4:13-22) verse 6 David the father of Solomon, whose mother had been Uriah's wife. (Bathsheba- 2 Samuel 11:1-13:38)

This lineage follows through from God's initial covenant with Abraham we first read about in Genesis 12: "I will make you into a great nation and I will bless you."

Annunciation and Birth

We must never lose sight of the awesome experiences that are unfolded in the Gospels concerning the announcement to Mary that "she was found to be with child from the Holy Spirit." (Mt 1:18) This was, as stated, the fulfillment of the prophecy announced by Isaiah in Isaiah 7:14 (NIV) "Therefore, the Lord himself will give you a sign: The virgin will be with child and will give birth to a son, and will call him Immanuel."

Luke expands on the visit of the angel Gabriel to Mary, and you can pick up the full record in Luke 1:26-38. Luke records that Mary is to call the baby Jesus, and he also tells Mary that "He will be great, and will be called the Son of the Most High."

Mary must have exhibited a certain holiness and godliness about her attitude for God to select her to bear his son, and it is a good exercise to think through her reaction to hearing this announcement (greatly troubled), but her conclusion in Luke 1:38: "I am the servant of the Lord; 'Let it be with me according to your word.'"

Luke also writes of the forthcoming birth of John the Baptist and in a scene that was to be repeated with Mary, the announcement was made by the angel Gabriel, who "stands in the presence of God." Because of his expression of doubt, Zechariah (John's father) was struck dumb until the child was born. You can pick up the full record in Luke 1:5-25 and

1:57-80. When Zechariah wrote on a writing tablet, "His name is John," to everyone's astonishment He regained his speech.

Mary's song in Luke 1:66-55 and Zechariah's song in Luke 1:67-79 contain wonderful prophetic words that showed the Holy Spirit speaking through them.

While you are reading these accounts, think of the geography of the area concerned. Mary was in Nazareth and Ein Karem where Elizabeth lived was about a distance of 100km. For a pregnant lady to walk that distance we would be looking at a three to four day journey. Keep this in mind when you remember for Mary to give birth to Jesus, Bethlehem was further, so we are looking at a journey of around five days. It is also hilly country.

Mary stayed with Elizabeth for three months and then returned home (Luke 1:56), another three to four day journey and three months further into her pregnancy. The Bible records this as so matter of fact. There is no mention of how she returned home. Did her new husband Joseph stay with her in Judea, or was he back in Nazareth working? Did she travel as a part of a group of people for safety, and did she sleep beside the road or in a small inn along the way? Knowing what we know about hydration, did she carry water with her, or what provisions were carried on such a trek?

A few months later it is time for the birth, but it is also timed for the census decreed by Caesar Augustus and so the journey from Nazareth to Bethlehem is made. We read that "while they were there, the time came for her to deliver her child," (Luke 2:6) but how long were they there in Bethlehem? Bethlehem is a little further than where Zechariah lived in the Judean hills, so we are looking at a longer journey of around five to seven days, allowing for the comfort of the expectant mother. In December the weather is likely to be wet and windy and a temperature range from around 10 C to 15 C. It is probably not the most favourable conditions for a heavily pregnant lady to make with a combination of walking and possible riding on the back of a donkey, sleeping rough and with minimal food and water.

And now for the media release – headlines in every paper around the world, Twitter and Facebook pages aglow. The long awaited arrival of Jesus Christ, the long awaited Messiah has arrived to "save the world". In an underwritten way this is what we read in the Gospels –

Matthew 1:24-25: "When Joseph awoke from sleep, he did as the angel of the Lord commanded him; he took her as his wife, but had no marital relations with her until she had borne a son; and he named him Jesus."

There is no mention at all in Mark's gospel – he starts straight in to the account of John the Baptist, and Jesus is not mentioned until it is time for him to start his ministry.

Luke 2:6-7: "While they were there, the time came for her to deliver her child. And she gave birth to her firstborn son and wrapped him in bands of cloth, and laid him in a manger, because there was no place for them in the inn."

John starts with some theological statements and then John the Baptist gets a mention. Nothing at all to start about Jesus' birth, but some very important background understanding of Jesus' role.

Yet the world goes completely over the top with its celebration of this event. "Christmas is a time for sharing," you hear; or "Christmas is for families". For many, Christmas is a time for the memory of heartache and sadness and loss of things that might have been. The world explodes with decorations, tinsel and lights and in hot climates such as Australia, cards are adorned with snow covered cottages and forests. Many object to the commercialism that is associated with this season, but at the same time go on buying sprees for Christmas gifts.

I don't want to be a Christmas Grinch and I do enjoy the celebration of Christmas and the reminder of this wonderful event. I do enjoy singing Christmas Carols and think that if people just stopped for a moment to take in the words they are singing, there would be no confusion about the meaning of Christmas. Take the carol "Hark the Herald Angels Sing", for example.

Hark! The herald angels sing: "Glory to the newborn King! Peace on earth and mercy mild **God and sinners reconciled**" and in the third verse:

Mild He lays His glory by **Born that man no more may die.** Born to raise the sons of earth **Born to give them second birth** Hark! The herald angels sing: "Glory to the newborn King!"

But one of the saddest verses in the Bible is found in the beginning of John's Gospel:

"The true light, which enlightens everyone, was coming into the world. He was in the world, and the world came into being through him; yet the world did not know him. He came to what was his own, and his own people did not accept him. But to all who received him, who believed in his name, he gave power to become children of God, who were born, not of blood or of the will of the flesh or of the will of man, but of God." (John 1:9-13)

Reject Jesus or accept Jesus? The King of all creation can be rejected, if that is our choice. From my personal perspective, that is so hard to imagine or fathom, yet that is the choice of millions of people living on earth today, and millions who have gone before.

The song says something about light. "Light and life to all He brings", but read the first few verses. "The true light". Many people seek for "enlightenment". What better source than the one who is recorded as "the true light"? We have discussed God is the Creator, the Spirit who "spoke" and created everything in an order that makes it all work to sustain life. We have mentioned that Jesus was part of this creation, and I have already mentioned these verses from Colossians 1:15-20.

The Supremacy of Christ

"He (Jesus) is the image of the invisible God, the firstborn of all creation; for in him all things in heaven and on earth were created, things visible and invisible, whether thrones or dominions or rulers or powers—all things have been created through him and for him. He himself is before all things, and in him all things hold together. He is the head of the body, the church; he is the beginning, the firstborn from the dead, so that he might come to have first place in everything. For in him all the fullness of God was pleased to dwell, and through him God was pleased to reconcile to himself all things, whether on earth or in heaven, by making peace through the blood of his cross."

So, mixed with this beautiful celebration of Jesus' birth, Jesus, who was a part of creation where "all things have been created through him and for him," came to earth and "the world did not recognize him." In many ways today, the world still does not recognize Jesus as the Christ, the Messiah, the Son of God. Verse 11 of John 1 goes one step lower: "He came to that which was his own, but his own did not receive him."

Earmark this discussion – we need to return to it later.

The Presentation in the Temple in Jerusalem

Angels have sung, wise men have paid homage, shepherds have followed the star, and at eight days old, as was the Jewish custom initiated through Moses, Jesus was circumcised and Mary had to wait thirty-three days to be purified from her bleeding. These were the rules established by God through Moses and we can pick up the process in Leviticus 12 from verse 6.

"When the days of her purification are completed, whether for a son or for a daughter, she shall bring to the priest at the entrance of the tent of meeting a lamb in its first year for a burnt offering, and a pigeon or a turtledove for a sin offering. He shall offer it before the Lord, and make atonement on her behalf; then she shall be clean from her flow of blood. This is the law for her who bears a child, male or female. If she cannot afford a sheep, she shall take two turtledoves or two pigeons, one for a burnt offering and the other for a sin offering; and the priest shall make atonement on her behalf, and she shall be clean."

Luke records that the requirement was "a pair of doves or two young pigeons." That is the sacrifice for a person who cannot afford a lamb. Mary and Joseph, Jesus' earthly parents, parents of the creator of the universe, who owns the cattle on a thousand hills about whom the psalmist sings in Psalm 50, presented the poor person's offering of a pair of doves.

Psalm 50:7-12

"Hear, O my people, and I will speak,
O Israel, I will testify against you.
I am God, your God.
Not for your sacrifices do I rebuke you;
your burnt offerings are continually before me.

I will not accept a bull from your house,
> or goats from your folds.

For every wild animal of the forest is mine,
> the cattle on a thousand hills.

I know all the birds of the air,
> and all that moves in the field is mine.

If I were hungry, I would not tell you,
> for the world and all that is in it is mine."

Recognition of the baby Jesus

We meet a couple of righteous and devout people during this time at the temple. Catch the narrative in Luke 2: 25-38. Simeon had a revelation that he would not die before he had seen the Lord Jesus Christ. Can you step into his shoes for a moment and imagine what that revelation would mean to you – a righteous and devout worshipper? A man obviously well versed in the writings of the Old Testament with an intimate knowledge of the prophecies of the prophets about the coming of a Redeemer, the Lord Jesus Christ, inspired by the Spirit of God. Imagine his reaction when he sees two poor peasant people entering the temple courts with two doves to make an atoning sacrifice on the birth of their baby boy.

Simeon, you are about to meet the infant Jesus who has been planning to visit the earth since before the creation of time. The Song of Simeon is worth repeating here. Luke 2:29-32: "Master, now you are dismissing your servant in peace, according to your word; for my eyes have seen your salvation, which you have prepared in the presence of all peoples, a light for revelation to the Gentiles and for glory to your people Israel."

The beautiful language of the King James Version of the Bible puts the first verse differently. "Lord, now lettest thou thy servant depart in peace, according to thy word:" (KJV)

Simeon says, 'Lord I am happy now to die!' What a privilege this man shared. And pause for a moment to think of Joseph and Mary's reaction. The child's father and mother marveled at what was being said about him.

But Simeon wasn't the only privileged one. The prophetess, Anna, who was widowed after seven years of marriage and is now 84 years old, having never left the temple, but worshipped day and night fasting and praying. Around 60 years this godly lady had worshipped the God of Abraham, Isaac and Jacob and being a prophetess was attuned to the leading of God's spirit. She also approached the new parents at that very moment and spoke about the child to all who were looking forward to the redemption of Jerusalem.

So we know that Jesus is just over one month old, and Luke jumps a few years into Jesus' boyhood.

The flight to Egypt

Only the Gospel of Matthew records this event linked to local historical detail. In Christian tradition, the wise men from the east came to worship the "King of the Jews". They had asked, "Where is the one who has been born king of the Jews? We have seen his star in the east and have come to worship him." (Matthew 2:2) King Herod, it is reported, was "disturbed" and on learning that the Christ was to be born in Bethlehem in Judea, started to institute a way to search for this child, and in a clumsy bit of espionage, suggested to the wise men that he would like to find the child to also worship him. The God of heaven (no plan of yours can be thwarted – Job 42:1) warned the wise men in a dream not to report the child's whereabouts to Herod. In another dream, Joseph was warned, "Get up, take the child and his mother and escape to Egypt." (Matthew 2:13) Egypt was a logical place to take refuge, as it was outside the dominions of King Herod, but it was still a part of the Roman Empire with Pax Romana – peace at all costs – enforced by Roman rulers.

Jesus' age is hard to determine. From about two months old to two years old, depending on sources and calculations, and suddenly he is about to be carried to Egypt from Jerusalem, a distance of around 520 km, or a travelling time of at least three weeks. The main route was a popular and well-frequented trade route – the Via Maris – and the safest way to travel would have been to link with a travelling caravan that would offer some form of safety and security, and possibly transport for Mary and Jesus, but nothing is said.

I also think about practical issues like food and water and sanitation, and once in Egypt, a means of earning money to support the young family. Nothing is written and it is only tradition that suggests where the family stayed in Egypt. It is almost as if this period is inconsequential to the main story of God's Plan A and Joseph and Mary just attended to it, as you do.

The horrible result of Herod being tricked into missing Jesus was the massacre of infants, where he gave orders to murder boys in and around Bethlehem up to two years of age. This is one of the figures put forward to why Jesus may have been two years of age at the time of his escape, or that it took Herod two years to work out the situation. The return from Egypt to Israel, specifically Nazareth, was after Herod died, but the situation was still tense, with the reign of his son Herod Archelaus.

The Forgotten Years

There is a blank page with no chance of entering anything onto it for the next few years. There is no mention of any marriage ceremony between Joseph and Mary, nor any records of the birth of Jesus' siblings. The next time we learn something of the young Jesus is when he was twelve years old.

It was a family routine: walk the distance from Nazareth to Jerusalem to the appropriate feast to be an obedient Jewish person, then walk home. Keep in mind this is a four day journey and for safety, there would have been a rather large group of family and friends walking together. Read the incident in Luke 2:41-52 and note a couple of things. Joseph was still alive, but there is no mention of any siblings. While Mary had in the early days been addressed by angelic presence, the normal day-to-day comings and goings of life are just that: normal comings and goings. When it was noticed (possibly the first night's camp) that Jesus was not with them, there was a time of concern, so they retraced their steps. For three days there were two worried parents anxiously walking through the streets of Jerusalem looking for a twelve year-old boy. No angelic vision this time saying, "Do not fear, Mary."

Why would you even think that Jesus, at the age of twelve, could be in the temple courts? A Jewish boy's coming of age is thirteen years, when he becomes accountable for his actions and becomes a bar mitzvah – son of commandment.

How does Jesus get to the stage of an understanding of the answers given to the teachers such that everyone is amazed? The 100% human Jesus would have been schooled in a normal education along with his Jewish heritage, but the 100% God within would have also given him the Spirit's enlightenment. There is no definitive answer to this conundrum, nor is there a need to be. But Jesus asks the question: "Didn't you know I had to be in my Father's house?" The King James Version asks, "And he said unto them, How is it that ye sought me? wist ye not that I must be about my Father's business?'"

Mary and Joseph had been Jesus' parents for twelve years. They had the memory of the angelic visitation announcing Jesus' birth. Mary had visited Elizabeth and was told of her baby leaping in the womb. Angelic hosts heralded the birth and shepherds and wise men visited from afar. There had been angelic warnings that necessitated the journey to Egypt, yet Mary and Joseph still did not understand Jesus' answer, but "treasured all these things in her heart."

Verse 52 is a fitting conclusion to this boyhood narrative: "And Jesus grew in wisdom and stature, and in favour with God and men."

The One Who Came Before

We have already met a cousin of Mary's in Elizabeth, wife of Zechariah, and without knowing who she was meeting, Elizabeth reported the leaping of the baby in her womb when Mary arrived pregnant with Jesus. After John was born, (the full reading can be read in Luke 1:39-45 and 67-80) all we know is that "the child grew and became strong in spirit; and he was in the wilderness until the day he appeared publicly to Israel." (Luke 1:80) The Gospel of Mark begins with the narrative of John the Baptist that is found in Mark 1:1-8. Mark offers a more graphic description of John's demeanour. "Now John was clothed with camel's hair, with a leather belt around his waist, and he ate locusts and wild honey."

I think you have to admit that he would have been a formidable sight. No means of washing, no barbershop to trim his beard or cut his hair. His physical appearance would have been daunting, but here is a man on a mission, a man strong in spirit and a man who knows his task.

His passion would have presented the passing parade of people with a dynamic encounter with a wild looking man appearing alongside them on the desert pathways.

What was his passionate message? Repent! Repent and be baptized! Turn from your sinfulness! There is one more powerful coming. Repent! He doesn't mince his words that we read about in Luke Chapter 3:7-18: "John said to the crowds that came out to be baptized by him, 'You brood of vipers! Who warned you to flee from the wrath to come? Bear fruits worthy of repentance. Do not begin to say to yourselves, 'We have Abraham as our ancestor'; for I tell you, God is able from these stones to raise up children to Abraham. Even now the axe is lying at the root of the trees; every tree therefore that does not bear good fruit is cut down and thrown into the fire.'"

"And the crowds asked him, "What then should we do?" In reply he said to them, "Whoever has two coats must share with anyone who has none; and whoever has food must do likewise." Even tax collectors came to be baptized and they asked him, "Teacher, what should we do?" He said to them, "Collect no more than the amount prescribed for you." Soldiers also asked him, "And we, what should we do?" He said to them, "Do not extort money from anyone by threats or false accusation, and be satisfied with your wages."

"As the people were filled with expectation and all were questioning in their hearts concerning John, whether he might be the Messiah, John answered all of them by saying, "I baptize you with water; but one who is more powerful than I is coming; I am not worthy to untie the thong of his sandals. He will baptize you with the Holy Spirit and fire. His winnowing fork is in his hand, to clear his threshing floor and to gather the wheat into his granary; but the chaff he will burn with unquenchable fire."

"So, with many other exhortations, he proclaimed the good news to the people."

John was quick to point to one more powerful than him was coming, one whose sandals he was not worthy to untie. John's offer was to baptize with water, but the one to follow was to baptize with the Holy Spirit. Baptism was not an ancient Jewish practice that formed a part of their culture and worship practices, but was something new. In the Old Testament, there are references to being cleansed with water, such as these two verses.

"I will sprinkle clean water upon you and you shall be clean from all your uncleannesses, and from all your idols I will cleanse you. A new heart I will give you, and a new spirit I will put within you; and I will remove from your body the heart of stone and give you a heart of flesh. I will put my spirit within you, and make you follow my statutes and be careful to observe my ordinances." (Ezekiel 36:25-27)

These are prophetic words that point to both the cleansing with water and the gift of the Holy Spirit. Throughout the Old Testament narrative, it is a rare occurrence where God mentions His giving or empowering of His spirit to people in situations needing that extra help. Since Jesus' time and the day of Pentecost, God's promise is to give the gift of the Holy Spirit to all believers, and this is given during the sanctity of baptism based on repentance.

King David's prayer of repentance in Psalm 51 also mentions the cleansing by water: "Have mercy on me, O God, according to your steadfast love; according to your abundant mercy blot out my transgressions. Wash me thoroughly from my iniquity, and cleanse me from my sin. For I know my transgressions, and my sin is ever before me. Against you, you alone, have I sinned, and done what is evil in your sight, so that you are justified in your sentence and blameless when you pass judgment. Indeed, I was born guilty, a sinner when my mother conceived me. You desire truth in the inward being; therefore teach me wisdom in my secret heart. Purge me with hyssop, and I shall be clean; wash me, and I shall be whiter than snow."

The four Gospels record John the Baptist's unique ministry — it could be called a pre-ministry. The location was Bethany beyond the Jordan, an area on the Eastern shore of the Jordan River that is now in the country of Jordan. Jesus came down from Nazareth — at least one day's journey, possibly two days of walking.

You may wonder why not much was recorded about Jesus' formative years. Throughout the Bible, I am amazed at the very detailed descriptions of some events, but the scant record on others. I have no answer for this, other than to accept that it is not important to the main story. Long distance walking, sleeping in primitive conditions probably on the side of the road, scant food and water. These are just accepted and at the time, nothing to really write home about.

The real story is about to unfold!

CHAPTER 5

THREE SHORT YEARS

I want you to think about the time scale that we are covering.

We started with Eternity – really there is no beginning to eternity and there will be no end.

In the beginning was God. There was a void with no matter that we understand matter to be. Over an uncountable number of earth years, each year just one revolution around the sun; the earth and universe took form under the creator's perfect plan. An earth year is the time taken for our planet earth to rotate once around our heat producing sun. Other planets in our solar system take shorter or longer times, and once we move into an understanding of the scale of the universe, (measured in light years) the time/distance measurement in space dwarfs our human habitation time scale.

The earth was formed and became habitable to living things and eventually not that long ago, in comparison to the age and time scale of the universe, the jewel of God's creation was formed when He breathed the breath of life into people.

Because of the wrong use of our power of free choice, as people, we started to want to take God from His rightful throne and remove Him as Lord and King of our life. This disobedience, this sin, meant banishment from God's presence, yet in the most amazing display of love and grace, this same God unraveled a plan, His Plan A, to bring people back to His fellowship.

From the beginning of the Bible, we can get a handle on some of the times involved, but the time we have spent most time talking about is from the time of the prophet Abraham, a person selected or called by God to be a father to all nations. Two thousand years start to be unwrapped and even in human terms, it doesn't really matter what time scale you choose to use, this is a relatively short period of time.

Two thousand years of history and Jesus came in an event that changed the calendars of civilization such that events before this Advent of the Christ and after it are classified as BC and AD. Before Christ and Anno Domini – in the Year of our Lord. The phrase is taken from the full original phrase *"anno Domini nostri Jesu Christi"*, which translates to "in the year of our Lord Jesus Christ". This has been modified recently to use the letters BCE and CE, meaning Before the Common Era and Common Era. The terms were made more politically correct and the terms completely overlap the existing calendars, and while it may appear to be modern, it seems to date back to 1615 and was widely used by Jewish religious scholars in the mid-nineteenth century. It came more into play in the twentieth century in academic and scientific publications by some authors and publishers who wished to emphasise cultural sensitivity to non-Christian people.

From four thousand years of history, we narrow it down to thirty years about which not much is recorded concerning Jesus Christ, Son of God, Saviour. In Sidereal (Planetary) time, Jesus' time on earth was about the same time that it takes the planet Saturn to go around the sun once.

We are now about to narrow this even further with three short years in the life of Jesus, from the age of thirty to the age of thirty three, the time of his ministry of teaching, preaching, healing and exhibiting his God-like qualities. It is from the four Gospels that we can learn of Jesus' time on Earth. There are many books written on the way the Gospels intersect each other in their recording of the things that happened in Jesus' time on earth, how they differ, their literary style, authorship and time of writing. It is not my intention to delve into this – remember this is a non-academic summary of the Bible. Each Gospel has material that the other Gospels do not share and there are many cross-over points and even common texts.

The Gospels' timeline is easily summarized into the following set of events:

- Jesus' birth
- His Baptism, temptation and the beginning of his ministry
- The early years – with more of an emphasis on deeds
- The culmination of His ministry – from Galilee to Jerusalem – emphasis on teaching
- The Crucifixion
- The Resurrection and Ascension

We covered Jesus' birth in Emmanuel, God with us and his boyhood in The Lost Years.

Baptism and beginning of ministry

Let us pick up where we left off in the last chapter with John the Baptist introducing to the Jewish world this new concept of baptism, which as one of the Anglican Prayer Book prayers in the service of baptism prays "sanctify this water for the mystical washing away of sin."[2] I am not encouraging a debate on how baptism is to be conducted, as there are almost as many cultural means of baptism as there are denominations. For our purpose in this book, please accept that baptism today is something that Jesus commanded us to do in his parting words before he ascended into heaven.

"All authority in heaven and on earth has been given to me. Go therefore and make disciples of all nations, baptizing them in the name of the Father and of the Son and of the Holy Spirit." (Matthew 28:18-19) What is important to stress is that baptism does not make us right with God on its own. The only thing that makes us right with God and gives us peace with God is our faith in the Lord Jesus Christ. We will come to this more fully later, but please understand that baptism *follows* our faith in Jesus. The church describes baptism (and other sacraments like the Holy Communion) in a manner first used by an early theologian, Saint Augustine in the fifth century as "an outward and visible sign of an inward and spiritual grace."

Jesus' baptism is recorded in the four Gospels, so it is good to capture some phrases from each gospel detailing the event. Jesus walked from Galilee to the River Jordan and we notice that John, recognizing Jesus' stature, tried to deter Jesus from being baptized by himself. Jesus, remember, is 100% human and 100% God, so in the fulfillment of his humanity, told John that it was "proper for us in this way to fulfill all righteousness." (Matt 3:13-17) John records, "The next day he saw Jesus coming toward him and declared, "Here is the Lamb of God who takes away the sin of the world! This is he of whom I said, 'After me comes a man who ranks ahead of me because he was before me.' I myself did not

---

2 *First Order of Adults Baptism. An Australian Prayer Book* 1978. Anglican Church of Australia.

know him; but I came baptizing with water for this reason, that he might be revealed to Israel." (John 1:29-31)

There would have been other people present during this time, (refer to Luke's account) but it is hard to visualize the scene. The actual baptismal words used by John are not recorded, but what comes next is certainly recorded, so it was heard by many. Elsewhere in the Bible we read of times that God spoke directly, described as a booming voice rolling across the heavens like thunder.

From the Gospel of John (John 1:32-34): "And John testified, "I saw the Spirit descending from heaven like a dove, and it remained on him. I myself did not know him, but the one who sent me to baptize with water said to me, 'He on whom you see the Spirit descend and remain is the one who baptizes with the Holy Spirit.' And I myself have seen and have testified that this is the Son of God."

From the Gospel of Luke (Luke 3:21-22): "Now when all the people were baptized, and when Jesus also had been baptized and was praying, the heaven was opened, and the Holy Spirit descended upon him in bodily form like a dove. And a voice came from heaven, "You are my Son, the Beloved, with you I am well pleased."

Matthew records (Matthew 3:16-17): "And when Jesus had been baptized, just as he came up from the water, suddenly the heavens were opened to him and he saw the Spirit of God descending like a dove and alighting on him. And a voice from heaven said, "This is my Son, the Beloved, with whom I am well pleased.""

Capture the scene and try to understand what your reaction to this pronouncement would be to hear this rolling, booming voice from heaven affirming this relatively unknown man from Nazareth. Jesus' baptism marked him out to be the Son of God. Baptism, as preached by John, was to follow and be accompanied by repentance. Jesus had no need to repent because of his sinless life, but it is suggested that as there were crowds gathering to be baptized, (and repent) his desire was to identify with sinful people. Luke gives us his age in Luke 3:23 as being thirty years of age and connects him with being the son of Joseph, "so it was thought".

The Temptation of Jesus

This next phase of Jesus the person's life is helpful to you and me as a person – the temptation of Jesus. This series of recorded temptations, possibly related to the apostles by Jesus, helped to define His Messianic role. Allow me to take a tangent from our discussions and head across to the book of Hebrews to see how important it was for Jesus to be baptized and tempted by Satan.

Hebrews 2:14-18: "Since, therefore, the children share flesh and blood, he himself likewise shared the same things, so that through death he might destroy the one who has the power of death, that is, the devil, and free those who all their lives were held in slavery by the fear of death. For it is clear that he did not come to help angels, but the descendants of Abraham. Therefore he had to become like his brothers and sisters in every respect, so that he might be a merciful and faithful high priest in the service of God, to make a sacrifice of atonement for the sins of the people. ***Because he himself was tested by what he suffered, he is able to help those who are being tested.***" (Italics mine)

It is also important for us to understand at this point that temptation is a common problem to us all. We read in 1 Corinthians 10:13: "No testing has overtaken you that is not common to everyone. God is faithful and he will not let you be tested beyond your strength, but with the testing he will also provide the way out so that you may be able to endure it."

In different translations of the Bible, you will find an interchange of words that may be confusing because translators go back to the original text that could offer various alternatives to use. Such is the case in these verses, where the word 'tempt' and the word 'test' are often interchangeable in other translations. As an exercise, try reading the above verses and substitute the word 'temptation' for the word 'test' or 'trial' and you will see what I mean. It is helpful to pick up the narratives of the temptations in the following Gospel verses: Matthew 4:1-11, Mark 1:12-13, and Luke 4:1-11. I have left these for you to read independently.

I want you to notice just a couple of things about the temptation of Jesus and by necessity I am being very brief on a subject that could occupy a full book. Leon Morris, in his commentary on these verses recorded in Luke, writes, "Satan began with Jesus' hunger and went on to raise a doubt as to his divine Sonship. Jesus had just heard a voice from heaven calling him Son (Luke 3:22). Satan suggests that he verify his Sonship by turning a stone into bread. The problem for Jesus was to know whether the voice he now heard came from the same source as the heavenly voice. His answer came from the Bible (Deut 8:3). What does not agree with Scripture does not come from God."[3]

I need to emphasise this last point –

What does not agree with Scripture does not come from God.

Jesus' temptation followed a period of "high" – his baptism and affirmation from God with a heavenly statement. His temptation played to his weakness because of fasting. The answer came from a Bible text – Deuteronomy 8:3: "He humbled you by letting you hunger, then by feed-

---

[3] *Luke*. Leon Morris. Tyndale New Testament Commentaries Volume 3. IVP 1983

ing you with manna, with which neither you nor your ancestors were acquainted, in order to make you understand that one does not live by bread alone, but by every word that comes from the mouth of the Lord."

From a different location we have a different temptation trying to appeal to a different aspect of Jesus' humanity – authority and splendour. Jesus' answer came from Deuteronomy 6:13: "The Lord your God you shall fear; him you shall serve, and by his name alone you shall swear."

The third temptation was in Jerusalem, so notice they did not all come at the same time, but possibly over periods of time. Jesus' answer quoted Deuteronomy 6:16: "Do not put the Lord your God to the test as you tested him at Massah."

Matthew records that at the end of these temptations, Angels came and attended him. Maybe you have experienced the love and care of a Christian friend at just the right time after some traumatic period in your life, or some strong temptations. It is a sobering thought to read in Luke 4:13: "When the devil had finished every test, he departed from him until an opportune time."

"An opportune time".

1 Corinthians 10:12 is a warning to be heeded: "So if you think you are standing, watch out that you do not fall."

Throughout God's word are many warnings and encouragements to us to be careful of falling into temptation. To some, the temptation is in-your-face blatant and it is very easy to determine right and wrong. However, for many temptations, Satan is very subtle in his approach to us and the "opportune time" that is presented may come over a period of time in many and varied ways. We will be discussing strong temptation, perhaps the greatest temptation, as we read about the time in the Garden of Gethsemane.

The Ministry begins

For many people who have not delved into the Bible, Jesus may be regarded as a good teacher, a wonderful person, and his philosophies of life would be ranked alongside early Greek philosophers such as Plato and Aristotle, or the German playwright and poet, Johann Wolfgang von Goethe, who has had numerous quotations recorded to his wisdom.

Jesus called twelve average type of men to "follow him", who, as we read, left everything and followed him. It is easy to read of Jesus' life as a narrative and you will find slightly different means of expressing the events in the different gospels and in some cases, what is recorded in one gospel is not recorded in another. Likewise, where and when Jesus walked is not easy to determine fully, but it is easy to find the pathways recorded in maps of the Bible land that show you where Jesus walked and where he performed the various miracles.

Please forgive me if you want to read more detailed descriptions of his ministry, but my aim is to keep pushing through our cryptic studies of Jesus and not the detailed studies. When you look at a map that details "where Jesus walked" you will see that his centre of ministry revolved around the Sea of Galilee and nearby Capernaum. There are records that state he visited Tyre and Sidon on the Mediterranean Sea coast, a distance of about 50km from Galilee (Matthew 15:21 and Mark 7:24) and whereas three Gospels account for only one trip to Jerusalem by Jesus, John records a number of visits.

In Matthew 11:2-5, we read, "When John heard in prison what the Messiah was doing, he sent word by his disciples and said to him, "Are you the one who is to come, or are we to wait for another?" Jesus answered them, "Go and tell John what you hear and see: the blind receive their sight, the lame walk, the lepers are cleansed, the deaf hear, the dead are raised, and the poor have good news brought to them."

In *Land of the Bible*[4], writing on the Miracles of Jesus, Benjamin Cronshaw writes: *"There are many miracles recorded in the Gospels including power over the forces of nature, health, daily provision and, above all, life and death. The ministry of Jesus certainly included many more that have not been recorded for posterity.*

"Jesus' healings are inextricably linked to his Messiahship. Whereas people were expecting a warrior-king, manifesting his power in military and political achievements, Jesus saw his Messiahship in the healing and wholeness he brought to people's lives. The kingdom he represents is not about dominance and conquest, but about healing and renewal. This was physical in healing their bodies and also spiritual in showing them the truth."

Jesus' healings attested to the fact that He was the Son of God and being the Creator certainly knows how everything holds together to work perfectly. While living on earth, to say that the Creator of the Universe, the King of Kings and Lord of Lords, lived a Spartan life would be an understatement. Luke 9:58 quotes Jesus' own words when a man had approached them to affirm he "would follow you (Jesus) wherever you go." Jesus replied, "Foxes have holes and birds of the air have nests, but the Son of Man has nowhere to lay his head." Only rarely do we read of Jesus and his disciples accepting hospitality, so for three years, Jesus and his disciples "did it tough", sleeping out under the stars and getting food wherever they could by whatever means they could.

I hope that you are getting an idea that there is more than one Eternal reason for Jesus to come to live on earth amongst his created order. There is the need for us to be reconciled to God. We need to have some channel of connection and communication with God to restore the original

---

4 *Land of the Bible*. John Cronshaw and Benjamin Cronshaw. Ark House Press 2017. The Miracles of Jesus

intention God had when he made us, but which was destroyed because of our willful disobedience – our sin – in the Garden of Eden.

Because of this sinfulness, human nature and all of humankind live in what the Bible calls a "fallen state". The ramifications of this fallen state can be found by reading Genesis Chapter 3, and in particular verses 16 to 19: "To the woman he said, 'I will greatly increase your pangs in childbearing; in pain you shall bring forth children, yet your desire shall be for your husband, and he shall rule over you.'

"And to the man he said, 'Because you have listened to the voice of your wife, and have eaten of the tree about which I commanded you, 'You shall not eat of it,' cursed is the ground because of you; in toil you shall eat of it all the days of your life; thorns and thistles it shall bring forth for you; and you shall eat the plants of the field. By the sweat of your face you shall eat bread until you return to the ground, for out of it you were taken; you are dust, and to dust you shall return.'"

In an earlier Chapter, I looked at the meaning and use of the term "cursed". It is hard to believe that nature is under a curse because Adam and Eve sinned against God. Humankind has done some wonderfully creative things in the pursuit of civilization and a better way of living, but there have also been some decisions made that have had negative effects on our living environment. Somewhere there is a happy medium that must be reached to improve the overall living conditions of people throughout the world, but we see the ramifications of greed and corruption in circumstances that are detrimental to the people affected.

So my question is: "Do you think that Jesus, in coming to live among us, also came with a plan or way to improve our normal living situation? Did He come to Earth just for Heaven for Eternity after we die, or is there something we can depend on for the here and now?" Let's examine his early ministry – the "doing" ministry.

The Here and Now

I am putting the cart before the horse here. Rather than put forward some arguments to reach a conclusion, I want to share my conclusion first and then examine why I reach this conclusion.

My conclusion is that I believe Jesus came to live on earth to teach us how we can also live on earth; to share how we can improve our standards of living and how we can live better in community. As a part of this improving our standards of living, He taught his Disciples (and we are they) things about how to lead a better life and how we can have a better character. It is a little of the "chicken and the egg situation", so let's start.

Assistance in living is not confined to individual living, but it extends to community. 2 Corinthians 1:3-4 states: "Blessed be the God and Father of our Lord Jesus Christ, the Father of mercies and the God of all consolation, who consoles us in all our affliction, so that we may be able to console those who are in any affliction with the consolation with which we ourselves are consoled by God."

What we learn from Jesus is to be shared. In community we are to encourage one another in our Christian faith, an encouragement that is for the here and now, but lasts for eternity. Paul's blessing to the Thessalonian people states, "Now may our Lord Jesus Christ himself and God our Father, who loved us through grace gave us eternal comfort and good hope." (2 Thessalonians 2:16)

Chapter 3, "Emmanuel God with us", spends a lot of time examining God's Plan A for both eternal values and temporal values. God's plan? Apologies for repeating this, but repetition is a great way to let things soak in. God's Plan A is in Jeremiah 30:22: **"And you will be my people, and I will be your God." For Eternity.** And while living on this Earth His intention is that we will grow to be like Jesus **"to be conformed to the image of His Son."** (Romans 8:29)

I need to get personal with you for a moment. The title of this book is about a Plan A or a Plan B for living. While God has only one plan, God's Plan A, as an individual person, you have a choice, and for most people the first choice, the human Plan A, normally does not include God in factoring in our life. I am reaching the pointy bit, the place where the rubber meets the road. If your Plan A for your life, the plan you have chosen to live, does not include God, may I suggest that it is at this point in our sharing that you need to consider making a change. I respectfully suggest you need to align your life with God's Plan A and make His plan your plan A.

Heeding the words of John the Baptist that echo in Jesus' own words, we are to repent of our sin and be baptized. We are to seek reconciliation and peace with God, a peace that is freely offered to us through the death of Jesus on the Cross and is very clearly stated in Romans 5:1-5. "Therefore, since we are justified by faith, we have peace with God through our Lord Jesus Christ, through whom we have obtained access to this grace in which we stand; and we boast in our hope of sharing the glory of God. And not only that, but we also boast in our sufferings, knowing that suffering produces endurance, and endurance produces character, and character produces hope, and hope does not disappoint us, because God's love has been poured into our hearts through the Holy Spirit that has been given to us."

From earlier chapters, words such as reconciliation, justified, peace with God, and grace appear, alongside an understanding of suffering – linked to temptation, trials and tests. These verses link our Eternal salvation with the development of a Godly, Christ-like character, a character that is to be sanctified and become more like Jesus.

So, if this is what God's purpose is in sending Jesus to live a human life, how were his deeds and teaching programmed to show this to us? What things did Jesus ***do*** in His ministry that either showed that he was God, or showed us how to live?

Miracles of God

Early texts and languages used in the Bible that refer to activity in Nature that were deemed to be supernatural in either their enactment or timing were referred to as a miracle. Other words used include wonders, signs, mighty acts or powers. The words used characterize God's involvement by His activity in human affairs and include distinctive, wonderful, mighty, powerful, meaningful and significant.

Miracles and the Natural Order

Miracles are events that dramatically reveal the living, personal nature of God who is living and active in human history, personally and purposefully acting out His purposes of redemption in the day-to-day living affairs of people.

In the OT narrative, we read of numerous "miracles" or "supernatural events" that occurred. Many skeptics try to link natural phenomena to these events as a means of explaining them away, but even with the natural occurrences, it does not alter the specific timing that the event happened, when it needed to happen, or when prophets inspired by the Spirit of God said they would happen.

I will list a few miracles and events that characterize God's activities as distinctive and wonderful, mighty and powerful. They are events that led to neighbouring and enemy tribes to express their fear of the God of the Israelites being on the side of the Israelite Nation, and hence against themselves.

The Call of Moses – the burning bush	Exodus 3
The parting of the Red Sea	Exodus 13:17 through to Exodus 14:31
Water from the Rock	Exodus 17
Joshua and Jericho	Joshua Ch 3 to Ch 6
Deborah and Barak	Judges Ch 4 – Ch 5
Star of Bethlehem	Luke 2:8-20 / Matthew 2:7-12

Jesus' performance of miracles of nature all contributed to the people's wonderment of his being a prophet or a messenger from God. While the early part of Jesus' ministry focused on his deeds, it also involved teaching, and often teaching using the performance of the miracle emphasised a teaching point.

Jesus' miracles involving the natural order

There is a conundrum here. Do you remember when we read about the Temptations of Jesus? Satan suggested that to cure his hunger, Jesus could command these stones to become bread? (Luke 4:1-6) Jesus' answer involved his quoting from Deuteronomy 8:3, where the Israelites were reminded that, while God fed them with manna rained down from heaven, they were not to rely on living on bread alone. Yet, look at the amazing miracles that involved the provision of food. Early in the ministry and before the calling of the Disciples, there is the situation on the shore of the Sea of Galilee where Simon was told to cast his net on the other side of the boat. (Luke 5:1-11) After the Resurrection, when Jesus waited for the dispirited disciples to come ashore from a futile night of fishing, in a moment of Déjà vu, Jesus told them to cast their nets on the right side of the boat. (John 21:1-14)

Two incidents are recorded where Jesus fed five thousand people and another four thousand people. (Luke 9:10-17 and Mark 8:1-10) We read that Jesus had compassion on the gathered people and there was no practical way to get food for them in the circumstance. After the incident in Mark, we read Jesus using these examples as teaching points where they also were caught short of food. You can read about this in Mark 8:14-21, with His questions and the warning to "Watch out for the yeast of the Pharisees." (Mark 8:15)

Jesus walked on water (Mark 6:45-54) and stilled the storm (Matthew 8:23-27) to gather the response, "What kind of man is this? Even the winds and the waves obey him." He caused a fig tree to wither by a verbal curse. (Matthew 21:18-22)

Miracles over life and death

If there is something about living in this world on which we have to agree, it has to be that there will come a time when we will die. Some people have tried to put their bodies into liquid nitrogen to preserve them for a future time when medical science will bring them back to life, but no matter what our spiritual or philosophical belief, we know that we have all been born, and there will come a time when we draw our final breath.

Some Bible verses linked together support this concept. "Then the LORD God formed man from the dust of the ground, and breathed into his nostrils the breath of life; and the man became a living being." (Genesis 2:7) "Nor is He served by human hands, as though He needed anything, since He Himself gives to all mortals life and breath and all things;" (Acts 17:25) and "The Spirit of God has made me, And the breath of the Almighty gives me life." (Job 33:4)

The God of the Bible has given us the breath of life and it is only by the Grace of God that we continue to live. I don't think it is stretching the imagination too far to state that as a sign of His divinity, Jesus was able to bring people back to life, and also because of His own resurrection, shows that He has the power over death. The disciples were witnesses to these amazing events. I have recorded two.

A Girl Restored to Life and a Woman Healed. (Mark 5:21-43)

"When Jesus had crossed again in the boat to the other side, a great crowd gathered around him; and he was by the sea. Then one of the leaders of the synagogue named Jairus came and, when he saw him, fell at his feet and begged him repeatedly, 'My little daughter is at the point of death. Come and lay your hands on her, so that she may be made well, and live.' So he went with him.

"And a large crowd followed him and pressed in on him. Now there was a woman who had been suffering from hemorrhages for twelve years. She had endured much under many physicians, and had spent all that she had; and she was no better, but rather grew worse. She had heard about Jesus, and came up behind him in the crowd and touched his cloak, for she said, 'If I but touch his clothes, I will be made well.' Immediately her hemorrhage stopped; and she felt in her body that she was healed of her disease. Immediately aware that power had gone forth from him, Jesus turned about in the crowd and said, 'Who touched my clothes?' And his disciples said to him, You see the crowd pressing in on you; how can you say, 'Who touched me?'" He looked all around to see who had done it. But the woman, knowing what had happened to her, came in fear and trembling, fell down before him, and told him the whole truth. He said to her, 'Daughter, your faith has made you well; go in peace, and be healed of your disease.'

"While he was still speaking, some people came from the leader's house to say, "Your daughter is dead. Why trouble the teacher any further?" But overhearing what they said, Jesus said to the leader of the synagogue, 'Do not fear, only believe.' He allowed no one to follow him except Peter, James, and John, the brother of James. When they came to the house of the leader of the synagogue, he saw a commotion, people weeping and wailing loudly. When he had entered, he said to them, "Why do you make a commotion and weep? The child is not dead but sleeping." And they laughed at him. Then he put them all outside, and took the child's father and mother and those who were with him, and went in where the child was. He took her by the hand and said to her, '*Talitha cum*,' which means, 'Little girl, get up!' And immediately the girl got up and began to walk about (she was twelve years of age). At this they were overcome with amazement. He strictly ordered them that no one should know this, and told them to give her something to eat."

Jesus Raises the Widow's Son at Nain (Luke 7:11-17)

"Soon afterwards he went to a town called Nain, and his disciples and a large crowd went with him. As he approached the gate of the town, a man who had died was being carried out. He was his mother's only son, and she was a widow; and with her was a large crowd from the town. When the Lord saw her, he had compassion for her and said to her, 'Do not weep.' Then he came forward and touched the bier, and the bearers stood still. And he said, 'Young man, I say to you, rise!' The dead man sat up and began to speak, and Jesus gave him to his mother. Fear seized all of them; and they glorified God, saying, 'A great prophet has risen among us!' and 'God has looked favorably on his people!' This word about him spread throughout Judea and all the surrounding country."

It is this power over life and death that Jesus exhibited in dealing with people and in His resurrection that makes the Christian faith "unique". Unique means there is nothing like it – there is only one.

Jesus' Healing Miracles

We often think the term "holistic" is a modern term, but Jesus had a holistic approach to people and still has that approach. He cares for our body and he cares for our soul or spirit. His interest in our life is not just for heaven and Eternity, but he is a God of compassion, for the here and now. This is evidenced in situations where there were problems brought about by the Pharisees regarding the forgiveness of sin and associated healing.

This is made very clear in Mark 2 when friends lowered a paralytic man through the roof because of the crowds surrounding Jesus. His first thing he said was, "Son, your sins are forgiven." When challenged by some teachers of the law about his authority to forgive sins, because no one can forgive sins but God alone, Jesus then commanded the paralytic man to "Get up, take up your mat and walk." His teaching point? "But that you may know that the Son of Man has authority on earth to forgive sins..."

At the Pool of Bethesda, (John 5:1-15) a paralyzed man who had been paralyzed for thirty-eight years was asked by Jesus, "Do you want to get well?" That would seem to be a redundant question, but it shows that any encounter we have with the Lord is by invitation. People were lowered from roofs, ladies touched Jesus' garment, soldiers came through the crowds on behalf of their children, but all seeking Jesus' healing touch. To me it seems strange that any person would knowingly reject the touch of God, or knowingly reject the Creator of the universe.

There are numerous miracles recorded where Jesus healed blind people, deaf people, crippled people, people with skin complaints, people with internal anatomical complaints, mental and demonic issues. Combining two verses from John's Gospel, we read "Jesus did many other signs in the presence of his disciples, which are not written in this book;" (John 20:30). The other "But there are also many other things that Jesus did; if every one of them were written down, I suppose that the world itself could not contain the books that would be written." (John 21:25)

Jesus' Action on Prayer

Jesus was (still is) the Son of God. Jesus, as God, knows all things and has the power to do all things. Jesus could discern people's thoughts and their spirit and yet, Jesus the man spent much time alone with God the Father in prayer. By his example he taught the disciples about prayer, as he continues to teach us today, and by his teaching he also taught the principles of prayer.

Please understand this. Jesus, while 100% human and 100% God, spent time praying regularly with God the Father. He had a Divine understanding of the Scriptures and he was well aware of his destiny in life. He had command over sickness, infirmity and nature, yet he spent time constantly in communion with God in heaven.

There are numerous books written on prayer and I encourage you to read these. The greatest encouragement I can offer is to pray. Pray about everything that comes to mind because nothing is too inconsequential to bring before God. Let me, in this Coach Captain's Commentary on the

Bible, touch a few Bible situations and verses that may be of assistance to you in praying.

Arrow Prayer.

I write about this first because it comes in the Old Testament. It may be helpful to turn to this incident as narrated in Nehemiah Chapters 1 and 2. Understanding that Nehemiah was "cupbearer to the king" and he was sad in the king's presence because of his understanding of the state of the wall surrounding Jerusalem, his life was at stake. In Chapter 2, verse 4 we read, "The king said to me, "What do you request?" Read this next section very carefully. "Then I prayed to the God of heaven. Then I said to the king..."

"Then I prayed to the God of heaven." No kneeling. No eyes closed. No hands clasped in prayer, and certainly no prayer mat. We are not told the text. What would you pray? "Lord please give me the words to say." "Lord help me." "Lord."

A quick, arrow prayer in a time of real need.

Gideon's worship

While still in the Old Testament, come with me to the battlefield, when Gideon was to face the Midianite army in an alliance with Amalekites and other eastern peoples. He had a depleted gathering of only three hundred Israelites. Turn to Judges Chapters 6 and 7 to gain the full picture. This is one of my favourite incidents recorded in the Old Testament as it shows God working His purposes through the weakest of the weakest. Pick up the narrative in Judges 7:9-15:

"That same night the Lord said to him, "Get up, attack the camp; for I have given it into your hand. But if you fear to attack, go down to the camp with your servant Purah; and you shall hear what they say, and afterward your hands shall be strengthened to attack the camp." Then he went down with his servant Purah to the outposts of the armed men that were in the camp. The Midianites and the Amalekites and all the people of the east lay along the valley as thick as locusts; and their camels were without number, countless as the sand on the seashore. When Gideon arrived, there was a man telling a dream to his comrade; and he said, "I had a dream, and in it a cake of barley bread tumbled into the camp of Midian, and came to the tent, and struck it so that it fell; it turned upside down, and the tent collapsed." And his comrade answered, "This is no other than the sword of Gideon son of Joash, a man of Israel; into his hand God has given Midian and all the army." When Gideon heard the telling of the dream and its interpretation, he worshiped; and he returned to the camp of Israel, and said, "Get up; for the Lord has given the army of Midian into your hand."

When Gideon heard the dream and its interpretation, he worshipped. He returned to the camp of Israel and called out, "Get up! The Lord has given the army of Midian into your hand."

(Italics for emphasis only)

In the middle of the enemy encampment that had camels too numerous to count, Gideon worshipped! No Hallelujah chorus. No shouting, "Praise the Lord"! No singing songs. Silently in the depth of the night and surrounded by his numerous enemies, Gideon worshipped.

Lord's Prayer

The best teaching of Jesus about prayer is the prayer we now know as The Lord's Prayer, and it is important that we understand its context. The disciples had been with Jesus for a couple of years and we read throughout the Gospel records on many occasions He and they drew aside to pray. Luke records an example of the disciple's prayer as they asked Jesus to teach them to pray. Their quest was effectively a prayer and one that we can emulate. In Luke 11:1 we read, "He (Jesus) was praying in a certain place, and after he had finished, one of his disciples said to him, "Lord, teach us to pray, as John taught his disciples."

It is expanded more in Matthew's account on prayer.

Concerning Prayer

"And whenever you pray, do not be like the hypocrites; for they love to stand and pray in the synagogues and at the street corners, so that they may be seen by others. Truly I tell you, they have received their reward. But whenever you pray, go into your room and shut the door and pray to your Father who is in secret; and your Father who sees in secret will reward you.

"When you are praying, do not heap up empty phrases as the Gentiles do; for they think that they will be heard because of their many words. Do not be like them, for your Father knows what you need before you ask him.

"Pray then in this way:

"Our Father in heaven, hallowed be your name. Your kingdom come. Your will be done, on earth as it is in heaven. Give us this day our daily bread. And forgive us our debts, as we also have forgiven our debtors.

And do not bring us to the time of trial, but rescue us from the evil one." (Matthew 6:5-13)

Gethsemane Prayer

We spend more time on this situation in a later Chapter, but as we are learning from Jesus something about prayer, I suggest to you that Jesus' prayer in the Garden of Gethsemane is the most important learning experience we will encounter. Capture the situation in Luke 22:39-46, but the key point I want to make here is in verse 42: "Father, if you are willing, remove this cup from me; yet not my will but yours be done."

Not my will but yours be done.

In using this prayer as a model prayer, what Jesus is teaching us, while praying for his own desire, is absolute and total obedience to God, despite the earthly consequences. Do you remember the first commandment? "You shall have no other gods before me." (Exodus 20:3) King of Kings, Lord of Lords, our side of the special, loving covenant that God has established is that He is to be God, Lord, Master. Our life, as we become more like Jesus, as we are "conformed to the image of His Son," is to learn to be obedient to what God directs.

The other teaching point of this prayer is the reminder of the need to: "Get up and pray that you may not come into the time of trial;" (NRSV) or "Get up and pray that you will not fall into temptation." (NIV, Luke 22:46)

Golden Bowls

In the last book of the Bible, the Book of Revelation, there is an amazing scene described about the great day of judgment, but it has a beautiful scene where we see the living creatures as described in Revelation Chapter 5. Verse 8 reads: "And when he had taken the scroll, the four living creatures and the twenty-four elders fell down before the Lamb, each holding a harp and golden bowls full of incense, which are the prayers of the saints."

Our prayers are special to Almighty God. They are so special that He treasures them in sweet smelling golden bowls full of incense for this great day of judgment and celebration.

Jesus' Teaching

We hear from many people who do not want to be confronted with the need to respond to the claims of Christ that Jesus was a "good teacher" and that he said some nice things. He is classified along with philosophers and other worldly acceptable "gurus". Jesus taught by example and his inter-relationships with people about living with people. He taught by parables and direct speech, which is plain to read and understand. He prefixed much of his teaching with the phrase, "he who has ears to hear, let him hear" and taught about the problem associated with spiritual blindness of those who have been blinded and are unable to see. His teaching, as we read in the Bible, is not just a matter of comprehension, but it involves an inner application to our heart and life.

There is a long-term application to Jesus' teaching and that is to prepare us to live with him for Eternity. This is a process that theologians call sanctification and it was mentioned in Chapter 3. God's concern, Jesus' concern, is for our character development. He is interested in our attitude to our fellow human beings, and particularly our attitude and obedience to God. Ephesians 4:1-6 captures this well.

Unity in the Body of Christ

"I therefore, the prisoner in the Lord, beg you to lead a life worthy of the calling to which you have been called, with all humility and gentleness, with patience, bearing with one another in love, making every effort to maintain the unity of the Spirit in the bond of peace. There is one body and one Spirit, just as you were called to the one hope of your calling, one Lord, one faith, one baptism, one God and Father of all, who is above all and through all and in all."

The fitting conclusions to Jesus' teaching as recorded in the four Gospels is best summed up by Jesus as recorded in Matthew 22:34-40:

The Greatest Commandment

"When the Pharisees heard that he had silenced the Sadducees, they gathered together, and one of them, a lawyer, asked him a question to test him. "Teacher, which commandment in the law is the greatest?" He said to him, "'You shall love the Lord your God with all your heart, and with all your soul, and with all your mind.' This is the greatest and first commandment. And a second is like it: 'You shall love your neighbor as yourself.' On these two commandments hang all the law and the prophets."

Saint Augustine is quoted as saying, "Love God and do what you like." Think about the ramifications of loving God with all our heart, soul and mind. And the fitting conclusion to a life lived by the teachings of the Master? Compare the two lifestyles that we find in the book of Galatians.

The Works of the Flesh compared to the Fruit of the Spirit (Galatians 5:16-26)

"Live by the Spirit, I say, and do not gratify the desires of the flesh. For what the flesh desires is opposed to the Spirit, and what the Spirit desires is opposed to the flesh; for these are opposed to each other, to prevent you from doing what you want. But if you are led by the Spirit, you are not subject to the law. Now the works of the flesh are obvious: fornication, impurity, licentiousness, idolatry, sorcery, enmities, strife, jealousy, anger, quarrels, dissensions, factions, envy, drunkenness, carousing, and things like these. I am warning you, as I warned you before: those who do such things will not inherit the kingdom of God.

The Fruit of the Spirit

"By contrast, the fruit of the Spirit is love, joy, peace, patience, kindness, generosity, faithfulness, gentleness, and self-control. There is no law against such things. And those who belong to Christ Jesus have crucified the flesh with its passions and desires. If we live by the Spirit, let us also be guided by the Spirit. Let us not become conceited, competing against one another, envying one another."

In this overall summary of what I am trying to achieve, this topic of Jesus' teaching cannot be covered in just a few words, nor can it be understood by any reader in the time taken to read this small book. Biblical scholars would agree that the study of Jesus' three years of ministry on Earth is a lifetime study and the application of his teachings is a lifetime of application. That said, let us move on to the Three Short Weeks to catch His Heavenly teaching.

CHAPTER 6

THREE SHORT WEEKS

In the previous chapter, I summarized the life of Jesus into six broad sections.

- Jesus' birth
- His baptism, temptation and the beginning of His ministry
- The early years
- The culmination of His ministry – From Galilee to Jerusalem
- The Crucifixion
- The Resurrection and Ascension

In this chapter we will look at these last three points.

The Culmination of Jesus' Ministry

Following a period of time ministering to people around the Sea of Galilee, Capernaum, back and forth to Jerusalem and also across the country to the Mediterranean Coastal area of Tyre, the emphasis changes from a ministry of deeds, or doing, to one of teaching. Neither concept was exclusive to the other, but the supernatural deeds performed and enacted in the first couple of years helped to show that Jesus had some form of Divine Authority, or his personal Divinity started to be qualified.

I have called this Chapter Three Short Weeks. I need to confess that this comes with it a degree of poetic licence as there are difficulties in establishing any timetable. We will read of two events and we can determine a timetable because the number of days are mentioned.

Peter's affirmation that Jesus is the Christ to the transfiguration. (Luke 9:18-36). In verse 28, we are told, "About eight days after Jesus said this…" Palm Sunday to the Resurrection was also eight days from the triumphal entry into Jerusalem to the triumphal overcoming of death in Jesus' resurrection.

So, counting Peter's Affirmation and the Resurrection, we do have two full weeks. In the Gospel of Luke, in the text between these incidents are many narratives concerning "on the Sabbath", but we are not sure exactly what Sabbath was being used as an example. Commentaries suggest the journey from Galilee to Jerusalem begins at Luke Chapter 9 and runs to the end in Luke 24. In between these two events is a "missing week", so while I am not suggesting the events in the chapters took place only in this period of time, I am book ending two important and significant events in the Ministry of Jesus around what really is an indeterminate period.

This time span, from Peter's affirmation and the experience on the mountain of the transfiguration, can only be described as intense and head spinning. Try to put yourself in the same position as the disciples. Your whole level of faith has revolved around the teachings in the synagogue, along with the strict regime of sacrificial offering and prayer and fasting. As a part of the teaching, you have learned there will be a Messiah to come at some time in the future, as forth told by numerous prophets. There was a degree of expectation that this Messiah would be able to free your Israelite nation from the tyranny of Roman rule, in much the same way that Moses freed your ancestral lineage, the original children of Israel. Just a few years ago, there was talk of the birth of a special baby called Jesus, whose parents lived in Nazareth, but then things went pretty quiet.

But through a series of circumstances that you don't fully understand, suddenly there is this mysterious person in your midst. A prophet, John the Baptist, has been wandering in the desert preaching a need for repentance – a strange type of man really, dressed in camel skin with wild and wooly hair. Some of your friends and relations were gathered around this John, who, when he saw Jesus passing by, exclaimed, "Look, here is the Lamb of God." (John 1:36) Other people began to be linked to this Jesus and a few days later, you, along with many others from your community, were at a local couple's wedding at Cana in Galilee. The strangest thing happened. The wine ran out and when Mary, Jesus' mother told him they had run out of wine, Jesus' answer was a strange one that you overheard. "Dear woman, why do you involve me? My time has not yet come." (Get the whole sequence of events in John 1:29 through to John 2:11) Then there is the strangest thing that Mary said to the servants at the wedding: "Do whatever he tells you."

And you experienced the miracle of turning water into the highest quality wine, the choicest of wine, and the narrative concludes: "Jesus did this, the first of his signs, in Cana of Galilee, and revealed his glory; and his disciples believed in him."

That miracle of nature was the first of numerous miracles to be observed first hand. Over the next three years, the disciples were to have their whole faith experience turned totally around as they experienced first-hand the amazing, clear teachings of this "Son of Man" and saw the raft of miracles of nature and of personal healings of many people and their relations, even healings from a distance.

Some "work experience" for the disciples.

Peter's Confession

It is a fair walk from the shore of the Sea of Galilee to a place that was once used for the worship of the god Pan, a Greek god who had a thirst for carnal pleasure. The region is identified in the Old Testament as Baal-hermon (Judges 3:3) and the spring of water is fed by the melting snows of Mount Hermon and forms the headwaters of the Jordan River. A problem with the pronunciation of the syllable P by the Arabs gives us the name today of Banias, and because of the natural springs, it was a place of refreshment and time for the disciples to pause with Jesus. We find this important confession of Peter recorded in the three synoptic gospels and I have written the account as recorded in Matthew.

Peter's Declaration about Jesus:

"Now when Jesus came into the district of Caesarea Philippi, he asked his disciples, "Who do people say that the Son of Man is?" And they said, "Some say John the Baptist, but others Elijah, and still others Jeremiah or one of the prophets." He said to them, "But who do you say that I am?" Simon Peter answered, "You are the Messiah, the Son of the living God." And Jesus answered him, "Blessed are you, Simon son of Jonah! For flesh and blood has not revealed this to you, but my Father in heaven. And I tell you, you are Peter, and on this rock I will build my church, and the gates of Hades will not prevail against it. I will give you the keys of the kingdom of heaven, and whatever you bind on earth will be bound in heaven, and whatever you loose on earth will be loosed in heaven." Then he sternly ordered the disciples not to tell anyone that he was the Messiah." (Matthew 16:13-20)

Jesus' question to the disciples was a direct, personal question. Let me say to you today that it is the same question he asks of each of us as a direct and personal question. "But who do *you* say that I am?" he (Jesus) asked. "Who do **you s**ay that I am?" (Luke 9:20a, my emphasis)

We have spent the time in this book searching for the answer to God's Plan A and its relevance to our modern life. This may not have been your intention, but I unashamedly made it mine. I wanted to be very clear in a non-academic way what the Bible is saying about Jesus Christ, Son of God, Saviour. For emphasis, I ask the same question that Jesus asked over two thousand years ago in the shade of the trees around this beautiful spring of water that continues to feed into the Jordan River.

"But what about you? Who do *you* say that I am?"

I need to leave off further explanation of this question until we come to Chapter 8, so let us continue with the gathering of Jesus and his disciples under the shade of the trees in Banias.

Some of the disciples suggested that people had thought that Jesus was some of the prophets of old come back to life, such as Elijah or John the Baptist. I have already mentioned that even today, some people say that Jesus was a "good man and a good teacher".

Peter, who has been close to Jesus for three years ever since he had his fishing boat used by Jesus on the Sea of Galilee, had heard many comments made about Jesus. At Jesus' baptism, he heard John the Baptist make a statement: "The next day he (John) saw Jesus coming toward him and declared, 'Here is the Lamb of God, who takes away the sin of the world!'"(John 1:29) and later: "I myself have seen and have testified that this is the Son of God." (John 1:34) In the record from Matthew: "And a voice from heaven said, 'This is my Son, the beloved, with whom I am well pleased.'" (Matthew 3:17)

Peter had been present on the occasions when the disciples had been confronted by demon-possessed people. "Let us alone! What have you to do with us, Jesus of Nazareth? Have you come to destroy us? I know who you are—the Holy One of God!" (Luke 4:34) And: "When he saw Jesus, he fell down before him and shouted at the top of his voice, "What have you to do with me, Jesus, Son of the Most High God? I beg you, do not torment me!" (Luke 8:28)

So Peter's conclusion?

Peter answered, "The Messiah of God."(Luke 9:20b). Matthew expands the answer a little. "You are the Christ, the Son of the living God." (Matthew 16:16 NIV)

I must pause here a moment to let the full impact of this confession sink in. The prophecies of the Law and the Prophets are starting to be realized. Jesus' presence on Earth and amongst His people is real. The witness of many miracles has started to cement Jesus' Divinity. The next thing that Jesus states is critical to our understanding of God's Word and anything related to our understanding of God.

"Jesus replied, "Blessed are you, Simon son of Jonah, for flesh and blood has not revealed this to you, but my Father in heaven." (Matthew 16:17)

Then as now, we need to ask the Holy Spirit to help us understand the things of God and this was the case of the disciples. God revealed Jesus to them step by step. What an amazing revelation! What an amazing thing to tell people.

But not yet. Peter and the disciples were told by Jesus not to tell anybody about this revelation. There was more to be learned in order to grasp the full importance of God's Plan A, but the conclusion is not far away. Between Peter's Confession and the next part, the entry into Jerusalem for my heading of "Three Short Weeks", I am guessing about this middle week. I think it was more than one seven day period, but for the sake of what I am trying to achieve, I am bookending this section of Jesus' life and ministry with the Confession and Jerusalem.

Jesus Comes to Jerusalem as King – the Triumphal entry

"After he had said this, he went on ahead, going up to Jerusalem. When he had come near Bethphage and Bethany, at the place called the Mount of Olives, he sent two of the disciples, saying, "Go into the village ahead of you, and as you enter it you will find tied there a colt that has never been ridden. Untie it and bring it here. If anyone asks you, 'Why are you untying it?' just say this, 'The Lord needs it.'" So those who were sent departed and found it as he had told them. As they were untying the colt, its owners asked them, "Why are you untying the colt?" They said, "The Lord needs it." Then they brought it to Jesus; and after throwing their cloaks on the colt, they set Jesus on it. As he rode along, people kept spreading their cloaks on the road. As he was now approaching the path down from the Mount of Olives, the whole multitude of the disciples began to praise God joyfully with a loud voice for all the deeds of power that they had seen, saying,

"Blessed is the king who comes in the name of the Lord! Peace in heaven, and glory in the highest heaven!"

"Some of the Pharisees in the crowd said to him, "Teacher, order your disciples to stop." He answered, "I tell you, if these were silent, the stones would shout out." (Luke 19:28-40)

Bad News before the "Good News"

Reading the Bible, both the Old Testament and the New Testament in the twenty first century means that we are reading with a perspective based on 2000 years of scholarship. Many Theologians have prayerfully garnered truths from the Scripture that were not evident to the people living in the times when they were written.

We have already discussed the "Good News" of the Gospel of the Lord Jesus Christ. In these next few weeks from Peter's Confession, Jesus will be dropping predictions and telling his beloved disciples that he will soon be put to death. It is during these next few weeks that Jesus will be teaching the disciples exactly what it means for Jesus to activate God's Plan A and the critical ingredient is his willing, voluntary death. We know this now because we have read about it and seen movies about the Passion of Christ. We have perhaps attended Easter church services where the story of Jesus' horrible death by Roman crucifixion is told and retold. But the disciples did not know what was to come!

Do you know how you feel and react when you receive bad news, either for yourself or for a loved one? Your head spins. You pray and pray. Nights are the worst because you wake constantly and try to pray, try not to think about the consequences. Eating is a chore. Well-meaning friends say platitudinous things to you. You smile and thank them, but you could almost scream. Nothing that is said is helpful or comforting because your heart and mind are not able to process much.

Step into the disciples' shoes for these next few weeks as they begin to go up to Jerusalem and as Jesus starts to repeat his predictions about his death. Note that these verses follow immediately from Peter's Confession.

Grab your Bibles and read with me these passages from the Gospels. At the time it was like a cryptic word puzzle, but from a historical perspective, we can see what Jesus meant about suffering, High Priests, three days and raising from the dead. This prediction is recorded in the three Gospels and it is good to record each version here. I am including these verses with little commentary as they are "stand alone" sections that bear reading and thinking about.

Jesus Foretells His Death and Resurrection (Matthew 16:21-28)

"From that time on, Jesus began to show his disciples that he must go to Jerusalem and undergo great suffering at the hands of the elders and chief priests and scribes, and be killed, and on the third day be raised. And Peter took him aside and began to rebuke him, saying, "God forbid it, Lord! This must never happen to you." But he turned and said to Peter, "Get behind me, Satan! You are a stumbling block to me; for you are setting your mind not on divine things but on human things."

The Cross and Self-Denial

"Then Jesus told his disciples, "If any want to become my followers, let them deny themselves and take up their cross and follow me. For those who want to save their life will lose it, and those who lose their life for my sake will find it. For what will it profit them if they gain the whole world but forfeit their life? Or what will they give in return for their life?

"For the Son of Man is to come with his angels in the glory of his Father, and then he will repay everyone for what has been done. Truly I tell you, there are some standing here who will not taste death before they see the Son of Man coming in his kingdom."

Jesus Foretells His Death and Resurrection (Mark 8:31-38)

"Then he began to teach them that the Son of Man must undergo great suffering, and be rejected by the elders, the chief priests, and the scribes, and be killed, and after three days rise again. He said all this quite openly. And Peter took him aside and began to rebuke him. But turning and looking at his disciples, he rebuked Peter and said, "Get behind me,

Satan! For you are setting your mind not on divine things but on human things."

"He called the crowd with his disciples, and said to them, "If any want to become my followers, let them deny themselves and take up their cross and follow me. For those who want to save their life will lose it, and those who lose their life for my sake, and for the sake of the gospel, will save it. For what will it profit them to gain the whole world and forfeit their life? Indeed, what can they give in return for their life? Those who are ashamed of me and of my words in this adulterous and sinful generation, of them the Son of Man will also be ashamed when he comes in the glory of his Father with the holy angels."

Jesus Foretells His Death and Resurrection (Luke 9:21-22)

"He sternly ordered and commanded them not to tell anyone, saying, "The Son of Man must undergo great suffering, and be rejected by the elders, chief priests, and scribes, and be killed, and on the third day be raised."

What the disciples did not fully understand was that Jesus was challenging them, as He challenges us today: "If anyone would come after me, he must deny himself and take up his cross daily and follow me. For whoever wants to save his life will lose it, but whoever loses his life for me will save it." It was for this reason that Jesus told Peter not to tell any person about his confession, that Jesus was the Christ, the Son of God. God's Plan A was only starting to be revealed. It was more than Jesus coming to live on Earth – it was integral to His suffering, death and resurrection.

I am jumping out of sequence here to read about Jesus' repeat of the prediction of His death as they neared Jerusalem. These warnings of his death were to be repeated in Matthew 20:17-19, Mark 10:32-34 and Luke 18:31-34. It is telling that Luke concludes Jesus' prediction of his death with the words, "But they understood nothing about all these things; in fact, what he said was hidden from them, and they did not grasp what was said." (Luke 18:34)

Let us go back to Caesarea Philippi and just eight days after Simon Peter's confession at nearby Banias.

The Transfiguration

For three years, Jesus was manifesting his divinity through the performance of miracles, through the lucidity of his teaching and by his general demeanour. At the beginning of His ministry at His baptism, remember that a voice from heaven affirmed that Jesus was God's Son.

Peter, in his personal confession of faith, identified Jesus as the Christ, the Son of the Living God. But this same person is starting to create an uncertainty amongst his disciples by predicting that some horrible things were about to happen to him and that He is destined to die. We now know why, but remember the disciples did not know what Jesus was talking about.

So Jesus takes Peter, James and John with him up to a mountain to pray. In Israel, there are two mountains suggested where this event may have occurred – either Mount Hermon, which is a bit further North of Banias, or Mount Tabor. Capture the narrative in three Gospels – Matthew 17:1-8, Mark 9:2-8 and Luke 9:28-36.

Jesus starts to pray. The disciples were very sleepy, but suddenly there is a heavenly vision and Jesus' appearance of his face changed, along with his clothes becoming as bright as a flash of lightning. Jesus was transformed rather than just being changed in his appearance and it is suggested that this transfiguration marks an important stage in the revelation of Jesus as the Christ in a similar way to his baptism experience. The appearance of Moses and Elijah suggest the law and the prophets are being fulfilled and superseded by Jesus. In the story of the Rich Man and Lazarus, the rich man, in conversation with Abraham, was told, "Besides all this, between you and us a great chasm has been fixed, so that those who might want to pass from here to you cannot do so, and no one can cross from there to us. (Full account in Luke 16:19-31) On this Mountain of Transfiguration, this great chasm is being breached visually, if not physically.

Arrival in Jerusalem

I mentioned that I am "bookending" two weeks of Jesus' short ministry period and condensing much of the middle week's teaching and activity between the Confession / Transfiguration and then the entry of Jesus into the City of David, Jerusalem. This really is "the week that was", a history-making period of time that continues to resonate around the world. Keep walking alongside the disciples as they in turn walk and live alongside their leader, Jesus. Your head is filled with so much teaching and memory of events. Your heart is in such turmoil about His predictions of being rejected, despised and acquainted with grief, the same words you have read in the Law and the Prophets. Crowds are gathering as word spreads that the Teacher is coming, the one who restores sight, makes the lame to walk, even raises some from the dead.

This same Jesus is the Manager of the events that are unfolding. Jesus seems to be initiating the events as if He is totally and absolutely in control of what is about to happen.

To express it mildly, this entry into Jerusalem was an audacious, "gutsy" event. Jesus and his disciples had walked from the Sea of Galilee to the small township of Bethany just to the East, and it is here we read of the death and raising of Lazarus, a friend of Jesus. (John 11:1-44) Some Jews, witnessing this ability of Jesus to overcome death believed, but others went to the Pharisees to tell them what Jesus had done. A hasty meeting of the Sanhedrin was called with the resultant decision that orders were given that if anyone found where Jesus was hiding they were to report the location so an arrest could be made.

> **Note:** The Sanhedrin was a Jewish tribunal or form of religious governance that was responsible for religious governance, but acted under Roman Law so was restricted under the conditions in which it met. It could exercise some degree of civil law but had to refer more serious matters to the Roman Courts.

In entering Jerusalem on a donkey, Jesus came, not as a Messianic conquering king on a white horse. The ass was the mount of a man of peace, a merchant or a priest, and while Jesus was symbolically stating he was coming as a Prince of Peace, the crowd was warming to the fact, as they saw it, the Messiah was indeed coming to rescue them from their imperialist enemy.

Each of the Gospels has a slightly different way of expressing this entry, (Matthew 21:4-9, Mark11:7-10, Luke 19:28-44 and John 12:12-19) but some of the expressions of the crowd echo the expressions uttered when Jesus was born.

We gain a continuing insight into the disciples' understanding of these events in John 12:16: "His disciples did not understand these things at first; but when Jesus was glorified, then they remembered that these things had been written of him and had been done to him..." Hindsight after the event is a wonderful thing!

The events of this next week zoom past in a blur of activity and teaching, coupled with the thought that sooner or later, someone will come from the Jewish leaders to arrest Jesus, but exactly when was anyone's guess. Crowds started to gather to celebrate the Passover in the Temple. With the crowds come the noise and mayhem of small streets, little alleyways, merchants selling their wares and selling things for the Passover. But what's this? Rather than keeping a low profile on entering Jerusalem and the outer court of the temple area, Jesus storms in to drive out those who were selling things for worship or for the Passover. Luke tells us: "Every day he was teaching in the temple. The chief priests, the scribes, and the leaders of the people kept looking for a way to kill him; but they did not find anything they could do, for all the people were spellbound by what they heard." (Luke 19:47-48)

Fast forward a few days to the eve of the celebration of the Passover. Again, note that Jesus is in charge of the preparations. Luke records that Jesus told them they would find a man carrying a jar of water – not a lady – whose role it usually was to carry water. When did Jesus arrange this? We are not told, but it is a part of the preparations made by him to establish the special celebration that Christian people have been celebrating ever since: the Last Supper.

The Passover with the Disciples (Matthew 26:17-30)

"On the first day of Unleavened Bread the disciples came to Jesus, saying, "Where do you want us to make the preparations for you to eat the Passover?" He said, "Go into the city to a certain man, and say to him, 'The Teacher says, My time is near; I will keep the Passover at your house with my disciples.'" So the disciples did as Jesus had directed them, and they prepared the Passover meal.

"When it was evening, he took his place with the twelve; and while they were eating, he said, "Truly I tell you, one of you will betray me." And they became greatly distressed and began to say to him one after another, "Surely not I, Lord?" He answered, "The one who has dipped his hand into the bowl with me will betray me. The Son of Man goes as it is written of him, but woe to that one by whom the Son of Man is betrayed! It would have been better for that one not to have been born." Judas, who betrayed him, said, "Surely not I, Rabbi?" He replied, "You have said so."

The Institution of the Lord's Supper

"While they were eating, Jesus took a loaf of bread, and after blessing it he broke it, gave it to the disciples, and said, "Take, eat; this is my body." Then he took a cup, and after giving thanks he gave it to them, saying, "Drink from it, all of you; for this is my blood of the covenant, which is poured out for many for the forgiveness of sins. I tell you, I will never again drink of this fruit of the vine until that day when I drink it new with you in my Father's kingdom."

"When they had sung the hymn, they went out to the Mount of Olives."

What a culmination of a week of strange happenings, amazing miracles, the far from clandestine entry into Jerusalem right under the noses of the Jewish Rabbis who were hell bent on killing Jesus, and now this strange Passover celebration where Jesus refers to bread as his body and wine as his blood.

The Mount of Olives is an olive grove directly across the Kidron brook from the walls of Jerusalem, overlooking the city. It was a venue well used by Jesus and his disciples and it was well known to Judas Iscariot, who was about to lead the arresting party to the point of betrayal.

The Garden of Gethsemane

I would suggest to you that these next twelve hours in the Garden of Gethsemane are the most important twelve hours in human history. I believe these hours are more important than the horrible day that followed when Jesus went through the process of the trial and his crucifixion, and I want to break it up into some bite-sized chunks.

- The Prayer
- The Disciples' response
- The arrest

The Prayer of Jesus

We have noticed that Jesus spent much of his time in prayer to God during his time on earth, but there was something different about this prayer. Let us look at the way each of the Gospels records the time of prayer. I wrote a little about this time of prayer in the previous chapter when I was writing about Jesus' examples in praying. This is such an important and integral part of the whole Bible narrative that I am writing the three versions of this time below.

Jesus Prays in Gethsemane

"Then Jesus went with them to a place called Gethsemane; and he said to his disciples, "Sit here while I go over there and pray." He took with him Peter and the two sons of Zebedee, and began to be grieved and agitated. Then he said to them, "I am deeply grieved, even to death; remain here, and stay awake with me." And going a little farther, he threw himself on the ground and prayed, "My Father, if it is possible, let this cup pass from me; yet not what I want but what you want." (Matthew 26:36-39)

Jesus Prays in Gethsemane

"They went to a place called Gethsemane; and he said to his disciples, "Sit here while I pray." He took with him Peter and James and John, and began to be distressed and agitated. And he said to them, "I am deeply grieved, even to death; remain here, and keep awake." And going a little farther, he threw himself on the ground and prayed that, if it were possible, the hour might pass from him. He said, "Abba, Father, for you all things are possible; remove this cup from me; yet, not what I want, but what you want." (Mark 14:32-36)

Jesus Prays on the Mount of Olives

"He came out and went, as was his custom, to the Mount of Olives; and the disciples followed him. When he reached the place, he said to them, "Pray that you may not come into the time of trial." Then he withdrew from them about a stone's throw, knelt down, and prayed, "Father, if you are willing, remove this cup from me; yet, not my will but yours be done." Then an angel from heaven appeared to him and gave him strength. In his anguish he prayed more earnestly, and his sweat became like great drops of blood falling down on the ground. (Luke 22:39-44)

Each account offers something more to the narrative. Luke, for example, mentions Jesus' sweat was like drops of blood falling to the ground. We get words like anguish, earnestly, overwhelmed with sorrow to the point of death, deeply distressed and troubled. Jesus knew the ordeal that lay before him as the sun rose, yet he also knew what lay before him after death – total separation from God because he was taking the sin of the world on his body. For the first time in all Eternity, Jesus would not be in loving fellowship with God the Father.

Unlike an animal about to be sacrificed as a blood sacrifice for sin, Jesus volunteered his life to Almighty God. It was at this point in time that all of Eternity comes together in the one pivotal point. Jesus agreed to "drink the cup of salvation". The day that followed, the agony of the crucifixion and the horrible death are all a consequence of this time in the Garden of Gethsemane on the Mount of Olives.

The two thousand years of history, from the time God called Abram from his home in Haran, from the long period of waiting and testing of his faith that was accorded him as righteousness. The connection of Joseph and his family to maintain the ancestral lineage, through the Exodus under the leadership of Moses. Through the period of time of the Judges, then Samuel, King Saul, King David, King Solomon and the protection of the Line of Judah during enemy exile. The four hundred years when there was no voice of any prophecy: this is the "pointy end", the place where the rubber meets the road.

Jesus Christ, Son of God, Saviour, the one who "was in the beginning with God and all things came into being through him, and without him not one thing came into being," (John 1:2-3) has come to the end of his earthly ministry and life on earth. He has come voluntarily. I can't say that word frequently enough. **Voluntarily**.

Before heading back to the Garden of Gethsemane to see the disciples' response and details of his arrest, it is essential that we pause to see the ramifications of Jesus' obedient and loving decision to "drink of the cup". In many ways, what we are about to discuss is the culmination of God's Plan A, the very reason for the whole story of the Bible – his story. It is too important to leave until what you might think is a fitting conclusion, so let us pause for a moment.

What is essential as you read the following is that we are like Peter when he made the confession that Jesus was the Son of the Living God. Flesh and blood cannot reveal this to us – it has to be from God's Spirit. It is not like English comprehension, but it is something you need to ask the Holy Spirit to help you to understand fully and to be able to take the message into your heart.

Psalm 119:18 is a good prayer to pray as you read this section: "Open my eyes that I may behold wondrous things out of your law."

In today's modern world, some would say "post-Christian world", we hear a lot about tolerance of other religions, accepting everyone's beliefs, freedom of religion, and the term "inclusive" to cover all forms of beliefs, creeds, lifestyles and abilities. It is important as I write to agree with the above statement about inclusiveness and acceptance, but at the same time, I have to stand firm, even dogmatic, on what I am writing because I am writing about the Christian's God. By the very nature of the term, Christian is about Christ. Luke, writing in the Acts of the Apostles, tells us that, "it was in Antioch that the disciples were first called Christians." (Acts 11:26) And the origin seems to stem from terms such as "soldiers of Christ", "the household of Christus", or "partisans of Christ".

In Chapter 2, I made a statement for my foundation of discussion. "The Bible is what it says it is, and God is who He says He is in the Bible."

- **Anchor Point #1:** There is only one God. The first Commandment issued by God to His chosen people as Moses led them in the Exodus to freedom was, "You shall have no other gods before me." (Exodus 20:3) When the prophet Elijah faced off the prophets of Baal on the Mountain of Carmel, his challenge then is the same today.

"How long will you go limping with two different opinions? If the Lord is God, follow him; but if Baal, then follow him." (1 Kings 18:21 – but I recommend you read the full narrative from 1 Kings 17 to 1 Kings 18)

- **Anchor Point #2:** Jesus Christ is the only way initiated by Jehovah God to bring people back to Himself – to redeem people. Jesus said to Thomas, "I am the way and the truth and the life. No one comes to the Father except through me." (John 14:6) "There is salvation in no one else, for there is no other name under heaven given among mortals by which we must be saved." (Acts 4:12)

- **Anchor Point #3:** You cannot save yourself – there is nothing any of us can do to make ourselves right with God. "But now, apart from law, the righteousness of God has been disclosed, and is attested by the law and the prophets, the righteousness of God through faith in Jesus Christ for all who believe. For there is no distinction, since all have sinned and fall short of the glory of God; they are now justified by his grace as a gift, through the redemption that is in Christ Jesus, whom God put forward as a sacrifice of atonement by his blood, effective through faith. He did this to show his righteousness, because in his divine forbearance he had passed over the sins previously committed." (Romans 3:21-25) "While they long for you and pray for you because of the surpassing grace of God that he has given you. Thanks be to God for his indescribable gift!" (2 Corinthians 9:14-15) It is important that I add some more sections from God's Word, the Bible that describes His plan of salvation and reflects why I repeated the voluntary offering of Jesus during his prayer in the Garden of Gethsemane. It is essential in the light of what I mentioned earlier about tolerance, acceptance and inclusiveness, buzz words of our time, that you note I am not making any commentary. What I am writing is straight from the Bible, straight from the God who reveals who he is in his Word, the Bible. I have highlighted some key verses that are essential to your understanding of this wonderful, unfolding plan of God.

- **Anchor Point #4: The Power of the Gospel** (Romans 1:16) "For I am not ashamed of the gospel; it is the ***power of God for salvation*** to everyone who has faith, to the Jew first and also to the Greek."

The Guilt of Humankind (Romans 1:18-32)

"For the wrath of God is revealed from heaven against all ungodliness and wickedness of those who by their wickedness suppress the truth. For what can be known about God is plain to them, because God has shown it to them. ***Ever since the creation of the world his eternal power and divine nature, invisible though they are, have been understood and seen through the things he has made.*** So they are ***without excuse***; for though they knew God, they did not honor him as God or give thanks to him, but they became futile in their thinking, and their ***senseless minds were darkened***. Claiming to be wise, they became fools; and they exchanged the glory of the immortal God for images resembling a mortal human being or birds or four-footed animals or reptiles.

"Therefore God gave them up in the lusts of their hearts to impurity, to the degrading of their bodies among themselves, because ***they exchanged the truth about God for a lie and*** worshiped and served the creature rather than the Creator, who is blessed forever! Amen.

"For this reason God gave them up to degrading passions. Their women exchanged natural intercourse for unnatural, and in the same way also the men, giving up natural intercourse with women, were consumed with passion for one another. Men committed shameless acts with men and received in their own persons the due penalty for their error.

"And since **they did not see fit to acknowledge God**, God gave them up to a debased mind and to things that should not be done. They were filled with every kind of wickedness, evil, covetousness, malice. Full of envy, murder, strife, deceit, craftiness, they are gossips, slanderers, God-haters, insolent, haughty, boastful, inventors of evil, rebellious toward parents, foolish, faithless, heartless, ruthless. **They know God's decree, that those who practice such things deserve to die**—yet they not only do them but even applaud others who practice them."

From Death to Life (Ephesians 2:1-10):

"You were dead through the trespasses and sins in which you once lived, following the course of this world, following the ruler of the power of the air, the spirit that is now at work among those who are disobedient. All of us once lived among them in the passions of our flesh, following the desires of flesh and senses, and we were by nature children of wrath, like everyone else. **But God, who is rich in mercy, out of the great love with which he loved us even when we were dead through our trespasses, made us alive together with Christ—by grace you have been saved— and raised us up with him and seated us with him in the heavenly places in Christ Jesus,** so that in the ages to come he might show the immeasurable riches of his grace in kindness toward us in Christ Jesus. **For by grace you have been saved through faith, and this is not your own doing; it is the gift of God**— not the result of works, so that no one may boast. For we are what he has made us, created in Christ Jesus for good works, which God prepared beforehand to be our way of life."

The Disciples' Response

This response is what triggered this book. Let us look at the reports in the Gospels that carry on from the prayers of Jesus listed above. "When he got up from prayer, he came to the disciples and found them sleeping because of grief, and he said to them, "Why are you sleeping? Get up and pray that you may not come into the time of trial." (Luke 22:45-46)

"Again he came and found them sleeping, for their eyes were heavy. So leaving them again, he went away and prayed for the third time, saying the same words. Then he came to the disciples and said to them, "Are you still sleeping and taking your rest? See, the hour is at hand, and the Son of Man is betrayed into the hands of sinners. Get up, let us be going. See, my betrayer is at hand." (Matthew 26:43-46)

"He came and found them sleeping; and he said to Peter, "Simon, are you asleep? Could you not keep awake one hour? Keep awake and pray that you may not come into the time of trial; the spirit indeed is willing, but the flesh is weak." And again he went away and prayed, saying the same words. And once more he came and found them sleeping, for their eyes were very heavy; and they did not know what to say to him. He came a third time and said to them, "Are you still sleeping and taking your rest? Enough! The hour has come; the Son of Man is betrayed into the hands of sinners. Get up, let us be going. See, my betrayer is at hand." (Mark 14:37-42)

Luke records they were "exhausted from sorrow", or "sleeping because of grief". In the Introduction I wrote about discussing this part of the Bible. As we discussed this passage, the question was raised about why they were exhausted from sorrow. The horrible time of the trial, the crowd's taunts and disdain, the reality of the crucifixion was all to unfold the next day, but even that was not known nor understood by Jesus' disciples. What was the sorrow, sorrow that caused exhaustion, coming from probably a week of fitful sleep?

The answer to that question is to read the chapters we have gone through in reverse order, taking note of the last few weeks when the whole of God's Plan A started to become real to those who had spent three years with Jesus. Why did he have to die? Why would he be betrayed? Why would he be delivered to the Gentiles to be mocked, spat on and insulted? This person who had healed people, who had spoken words so enriching that many followed with changed lives. This person who had been baptized and heard God speaking from heaven, to be followed by God speaking from the Mountain when he had glowed.

I detoured a little above, but notice that the things I quoted were all from books still to be written; books and teachings yet to be understood. What turmoil of mind and spirit the disciples went through during these last few weeks, and now after the strangest of Passover Suppers, when Jesus talked about His body and His blood. Exhausted from sorrow and grief to which we could add confusion, turmoil, uncertainty.

Try to picture the scene. Jesus' prayer to His heavenly Father was for obedience, knowing what was to follow; obedience to the practical outworking of the First Commandment. His team was fast asleep, offering no support at all. The spirit was indeed willing, but the flesh was weak, and greatly weakened. Jesus advises them to "watch and pray." Pray about what?

Did he ask them to pray for Himself? To support him in his greatest hour of need? Please pray for me so that I will be strengthened to face the ordeal ahead of me.

Did he suggest they pray for strength for the days ahead?

None of that.

"Get up and pray that you may not come into the time of trial."

What? In the pivotal, turning point of human history, when Jesus is offering His life as the "full, perfect and sufficient sacrifice", Jesus is concerned that His followers (then the disciples – today it is we his followers) will not fall into temptation.

We have touched on temptation earlier, something that happened to Jesus and something that will happen to us while ever we live. What is the greatest temptation the disciples were likely to face? It is the same temptation that we could call the greatest temptation we are likely to face in the twenty first century.

In the light of history, and our understanding of what happened to Jesus in the next day, what reaction would be understandable for the disciples, then and now?

To be flattened. To have our faith shattered. All the hopes we had for salvation from a Messiah are now in tatters. Give up! It's not worth the angst.

Without putting words into Jesus' mouth, but thinking aloud what his thought processes may have been, we could think that Jesus would be thinking "Tomorrow you are going to witness what will become the greatest sham of a trial that will ever be witnessed. You will hear false testimony from leaders of the faith who should never tell the lies they are about to tell. You will witness man's inhumanity to man as I am whipped and scourged, and you will eventually see me breathe my last breath."

"Don't give up!"

"Hold firm the things you have seen and heard."

"It is not the end, it is just the beginning."

These words were to be written after these events, but resonate with us in our day-to-day life, our comings and goings.

A Call to Persevere

"Therefore, my friends, since we have confidence to enter the sanctuary by the blood of Jesus, by the new and living way that he opened for us through the curtain (that is, through his flesh), and since we have a great priest over the house of God, let us approach with a true heart in full assurance of faith, with our hearts sprinkled clean from an evil conscience and our bodies washed with pure water. Let us hold fast to the confession of our hope without wavering, for he who has promised is faithful. And let us consider how to provoke one another to love and good deeds, not neglecting to meet together, as is the habit of some, but encouraging one another, and all the more as you see the Day approaching." (Hebrews 10:19-25)

In his book *"Encouragement"*, Author Larry Crabb writes, "We are reminded in Hebrews that difficulties along the path of obedience can weaken our determination to follow Christ – and therefore we should encourage one another. The thoughts in the Scripture passages seem to be that we are to motivate each other to walk with the Lord more closely, 'encouraging' one another to live out the truth of our position in Christ by loving others and doing good works."

He concludes his preface by stating: "A simply worded definition of encouragement might be this – *Encouragement is the kind of expression that helps someone want to be a better Christian, even when life is tough.*"[5]

---

5 *Encouragement.* Larry Crabb & Dr Dan Alexander. Zondervan 2010

The greatest temptation? Watch and pray that you enter not into (this) temptation.

Do not give up your faith. It has eternal consequences.

2 Thessalonians 2:16 states: "May our Lord Jesus Christ himself and God our Father, who loved us and ***by his grace gave us eternal encouragement*** and good hope, encourage your hearts and strengthen you in every good deed and word."

The Arrest

This is a crazy thing to understand. Jesus was absolutely, totally in control of his own arrest, trial and crucifixion. We have traced God's plan of redemption through his chosen group of people, offspring of Abraham and Sarah. We have learned of numerous prophets prophesying that there would come to live on Earth a Saviour for these people, and in fact, for all people. We have seen this man Jesus performing miracles that could only be linked to a Divine source, and we have heard of some amazing, positively revolutionary teaching. Revolutionary, not in the sense of being against the established government but in the manner in which we are to live with and treat our fellow human beings.

We have heard of His prayer in the Garden of Gethsemane that followed such a strange Passover celebration with his closest band of people. A prayer of submission and obedience to the Creator God, the God who has been with His chosen people, despite their wayward lifestyles.

And now we are about to witness this miscarriage of human justice that results in a horrible, agonizing death by slow suffocation in the heat of the sun.

Yet Jesus Christ, Son of God, Saviour, is totally in control of the events in the trial before Pilate that is to follow. We read of this exchange in John 19:10-11: "Pilate therefore said to him, "Do you refuse to speak to me? Do you not know that I have power to release you, and power to crucify you?" Jesus answered him, "You would have no power over me unless it had been given you from above; therefore the one who handed me over to you is guilty of a greater sin."

I want you to visualize the scene that you can read in John 18, the same scene in the Garden of Gethsemane we have just visited. It is early morning darkness when Jesus spoke with his disciples when they were sleeping. The Kidron Valley is a reasonably steep-sided valley outside the walled city of Jerusalem and opposite the city is the Garden of Gethsemane that leads to the Mount of Olives. We read that Judas led a detachment of soldiers and some officials from the chief priests and the Pharisees and they were carrying lanterns and weapons.

The Garden was an area that Jesus and His disciples frequented. Judas knew this and Jesus knew that Judas would lead the arresting party there because he had predicted Judas would betray him. Yet he made no effort to change the venue. "He (Jesus) came out and went, as was his custom, to the Mount of Olives; and the disciples followed him." (Luke 22:39)

This is not the type of action one would expect in a thriller movie, when the person betrayed knows of the enemy's plans, but walks right into their trap. From the slopes of the garden, they would have a good view across to the city gate from where the arresting party would come, torches in hand (nothing secretive here) and weaving down the pathway to cross the Kidron brook, then up the side of the Mount of Olives. Judas, in the lead wrapped against the cold, the High Priest, officials and Pharisees, along with a detachment of Roman Guards and Temple police. The guards would have been in full armour so their chain mail and shields, probably clanking as they walked, clearly audible in the pre dawn darkness.

Pick up the narrative in John 18:4-5: "Then Jesus, knowing all that was to happen to him, came forward and asked them, "Whom are you looking for?" They answered, "Jesus of Nazareth." Jesus replied, "I am he." Judas, who betrayed him, was standing with them. Judas' intention was to identify Jesus with a kiss. There was no need. Jesus stepped forward to state his identity with three little words: "I am he."

We have a detachment of people – some "very important" community people, some high-ranking temple officials and some burly soldiers ready for action. Men who would rather have a fight than a feed, as some Australian men would put it. Tough fellows, whose job was to be prepared to fight to the death using their brawn.

And what happens when Jesus said those three little words? When Jesus said to them "I am he," they stepped back and fell to the ground. (Verse 6)

Like a chain of dominoes falling, this very powerful, very important group of people buckled at the knees and fell to the ground. Imagine the mayhem, and the embarrassment. What about the soldiers debrief with their superiors once they were back in the barracks?

Once their composure was regained, and the soldiers dusted themselves off and tried to look menacing again, Jesus repeated the question, and not only did he tell them "I am he," but he also controlled the arresting party. "I told you that I am he. So if you are looking for me, let these men go." None of this aiding and abetting, or consorting with criminals…

Instead, "Yes sir, sorry sir, we will only arrest you, sir."

So the soldiers, their officer and the Jewish police arrested Jesus and bound him. "First they took him to Annas, who was the father-in-law of Caiaphas, the high priest that year." (Verses 12-13)

The horrible proceedings had begun, but Jesus was in command.

CHAPTER 7

THREE LONG DAYS

The ruling legal system

The Bible tells us that when the right time had come, God sent Jesus into the World. (Galatians 4:4) An examination of the history of the World will tell us that around this pivotal time, there were many large civilisations in the world, including the Egyptian Pharoahs, Chinese and Indian dynasties and the area surrounding Israel was under Roman rule. It is interesting to look at maps showing the extent of the Roman Empire during Jesus' time on Earth and the rule of Rome was more successful than previous occupations such as that from Persia. You would be aware of the conquering of the Israelites by the Babylonians under the reign of King Nebuchadnezzar that is clearly outlined in the book of Daniel. The greater population were exiled and taken to live in Babylon in slavery.

In later years, King Cyrus had a policy that he thought people would be more productive if they were able to have their own culture and religion, instead of something imposed on them, and he allowed the Jews to return to their own land in around 538 BC. It was this concept that the Roman rulers copied in their governance of the many conquered kingdoms throughout the shores of the Mediterranean Sea, but to keep the peace, a policy of Pax Romana was established. This was "peace at all costs," so any form of gathering or the creation of a disturbance was eliminated as quickly as possible.

The Jewish system of governance was established back in Moses' time and it was called the Sanhedrin. It was an odd numbered council of Jewish leaders who would meet to dispense with justice, particularly in regard to Jewish law, and the Roman Caesars allowed the Jews to maintain this in respect of their religious governance. A modern person could look at this and probably think that this Sanhedrin could be thought to be subject to and bowed to Roman rule, particularly Pax Romana, and I don't think you could be blamed for thinking that.

But you can sense the conflict of interest and the minefield that Jesus walked through with his teachings. His claim about fulfilling the law and replacing the law. His bending of the rules about the treatment of the rest day, the Sabbath. The mental gymnastics that occurred when Pharisees and Sadducees, many of whom were members of the Sanhedrin, challenged Jesus with their questions.

Coupled with this, you have the desire of the Jewish people to have come among them a "Messiah", one who would deliver them from Roman rule and occupation that immediately turns on warning lights in the secular rule makers responsible for maintaining law and order.

It is into this hot bed of political and civil unrest we find Jesus confronting the rulers of both the Synagogue and the Country. Set against this background of governing styles and processes we then also find the human interaction of the leaders who were trying to avoid any civil unrest and uprising likely to disturb the peace and bring with it the heavy handed Roman legions whose job it was to keep the peace – the old strike-first-ask-questions-later administration of justice.

Jesus' Trial

Have you noticed that whenever you read a report of a trial, or watch the interviews on TV of people directly affected by the offence, there is always a bias? There is a bias in the reporting and the content, there is a bias on the part of the people affected, whether they were on the side of the prosecution or the defense, and we have a natural bias. To take an example, if we were not in favour of the use of drugs and we witness someone being caught or tried for drug running or possession, have you noticed that you automatically side with the police and the drug enforcement agencies? If a person who is in favour of drug use watches the same report, their bias would show a different reaction.

When we read the various accounts of Jesus' trial in the Gospels, we read these accounts with a natural bias. I think it would be fair to say that for a Christian person reading these accounts, the bias would naturally go against the people who were putting Jesus on trial, or who were responsible for his handling. What I want to stress as we read of these accounts is what I wrote in the closing pages of the last chapter. Jesus was in charge of His own trial. From before the creation of the world and the wonderful creation of human life, Jesus knew that there would come a time when He would leave Heaven to live on Earth. There would come a time when He would reveal himself as the Son of God and there would come a time when He would be scourged, mocked and treated with contempt before He had to die.

The opening verses of John's Gospel summarise this in John 1:10-11. "He (Jesus) was in the world, and the world came into being through him; yet the world did not know him. He came to what was his own, and his own people did not accept him." There are many who blame the Jewish people for Jesus' death and crucifixion based on these verses. I have already mentioned that verse 11 is one of the saddest verses in the Bible in regard to our treatment of Jesus. I would like to suggest that today, anytime any one of us refuses to be obedient to Jesus, we are guilty of the same charge. If we choose not to believe in Him, we are rejecting him, we are not receiving him, and in the process we are rejecting God. This concept was borne in our readings in the previous Chapter when quoting Romans 1.

Luke 10:16 warns: "Whoever listens to you listens to me, and whoever rejects you rejects me, and whoever rejects me rejects the one who sent me." 1 Thessalonians 4:8 states, "Therefore whoever rejects this rejects not human authority but God, who also gives his Holy Spirit to you."

Our bias must turn away from putting blame on the Jewish people or the Roman officials, but we must share the blame because of our own sinfulness. The lyrics of the song, "How Deep the Father's Love for us"[6] contain the words: "It was my sin that held Him there Until it was accomplished," emphasises my role, our role, in Jesus' long, horrible three days.

It will be helpful to read the various accounts of Jesus' trial and pathway to Golgotha. Find them in Matthew 26:57 to 27:31, Mark 14:43 to 15:20, Luke 22:63 to 23:25, and John 18:19 to 19:16.

As you read these accounts, keep in mind your twenty first century bias based on the knowledge of what was to follow. Notice that Jesus spoke in answer when it was appropriate, but where it served no useful purpose, "He opened not His mouth, like a sheep before its shearers is silent."

This was prophesied in Isaiah 53:7: "He was oppressed, and he was afflicted, yet he did not open his mouth; like a lamb that is led to the slaughter, and like a sheep that before its shearers is silent, so he did not open his mouth." It was this prophecy that the Ethiopian eunuch was

---

6 *How Deep the Father's Love for Us* – Stuart Townend

reading when Philip caught up with him reading in his chariot on his long, slow return to Ethiopia from his visit to Jerusalem to worship. Read the full incident in Acts 8:26-40.

Jesus did not retaliate in his comments, but challenged the members of the Sanhedrin with his answer to their questioning statement recorded in Luke 22 from verse 67.

"They said, "If you are the Messiah, tell us." He replied, "If I tell you, you will not believe; and if I question you, you will not answer. But from now on the Son of Man will be seated at the right hand of the power of God." All of them asked, "Are you, then, the Son of God?" He said to them, "You say that I am." Then they said, "What further testimony do we need? We have heard it ourselves from his own lips!"

It was this charge of blasphemy that meant the Sanhedrin wanted Jesus dealt with in a further court, but they had no power of life and death over their jurisdiction. A "religious" complaint could not be dealt with through the Roman Court of Law, so when the Jewish leaders took Jesus to Pilate, they brought forth the charge of subverting the nation about taxation payments as well as his claim to be the Messiah, a king.

A casual observer would say that Pilate was washing his hands of the affair. In reality he was playing right into Jesus' hands because Jesus knew his fate was the Cross.

In another turn of events, Pilate, wishing to have the crowd release Jesus from prison as was the custom because of the Feast of the Passover, thought that the crowd would accept Jesus, who had done no wrong, instead of Barabbas, who had been imprisoned for insurrection and murder. But mob rule, inflamed by rabble-rousers and people with nothing better to do, shouted, "Crucify him, crucify him," and release Barabbas.

This godless rule of the mob of people who have chosen by their own free will to ignore the first commandment (You shall have no other Gods before me) and so have also rejected the Son of Man has continued to echo through the ages. Throughout the free world, the western World, or whatever term you choose to use, nations that had a Christian heritage in their foundation are fast turning from the God on whom they initially based their country's establishment. Legislation in most countries is being written that detracts from godly principles and standards, and democracy that is based on majority vote is being swamped by people who have no allegiance to God, or to Jesus, through whom they have received their life and breath.

And so the sinless Son of Man, Son of God, Saviour and Messiah is led to his excruciatingly painful death by one of the most visible and barbaric means of public execution known to people.

The Physical Agony of Jesus on the Cross

Please remember the facts about Jesus. He was a human being, subject to the perception of pain, the reality of hunger and thirst, and had physical limitations that he had no intention of stepping away from as was evidenced in his time of temptation. He was also God incarnate, and as God, knew the process through which He would be led to his death. This must have added a mental process that would have affected his physical struggle and the process of dying was "not to die peacefully with a smile on His face."

I think most people are aware of the process of dying by crucifixion. There is the agony of having nails hammered into your hands and feet, then having the cross dropped into position to add to that pain. But the real agony comes very slowly as the muscles of the body grow tired and cannot sustain the weight of the body, so breathing becomes harder and harder. Breathing is an involuntary action of the body, so it is almost impossible to stop breathing for any length of time before your automatic responses kick in. So breathing becomes painful against the pain of the nails, not breathing becomes nearly impossible. The breath that God gives is harder and harder to receive.

So we hear Jesus cry out *"Eloi, Eloi, lema sabachthani?"* (which means "My God, my God, why have you forsaken me?") It is important to have each of the Gospel's account to read about this event, so I have included the accounts in full.

The Death of Jesus

(Matthew 27:45-55)

"From noon on, darkness came over the whole land until three in the afternoon. And about three o'clock Jesus cried with a loud voice, "Eloi, Eloi, lema sabachthani?" that is, "My God, my God, why have you forsaken me?" When some of the bystanders heard it, they said, "This man is calling for Elijah." At once one of them ran and got a sponge, filled it with sour wine, put it on a stick, and gave it to him to drink. But the others said, "Wait, let us see whether Elijah will come to save him." Then Jesus cried again with a loud voice and breathed his last. At that moment the curtain of the temple was torn in two, from top to bottom. The earth shook, and the rocks were split. The tombs also were opened, and many bodies of the saints who had fallen asleep were raised. After his resurrection they came out of the tombs and entered the holy city and appeared to many. Now when the centurion and those with him, who were keeping watch over Jesus, saw the earthquake and what took place, they were terrified and said, "Truly this man was God's Son!"

"Many women were also there, looking on from a distance; they had followed Jesus from Galilee and had provided for him."

(Mark 15:23-39)

"And they offered him wine mixed with myrrh; but he did not take it. And they crucified him, and divided his clothes among them, casting lots to decide what each should take.

"It was nine o'clock in the morning when they crucified him. The inscription of the charge against him read, "The King of the Jews." And with him they crucified two bandits, one on his right and one on his left. Those who passed by derided him, shaking their heads and saying, "Aha! You who would destroy the temple and build it in three days, save yourself, and come down from the cross!" In the same way the chief priests, along with the scribes, were also mocking him among themselves and saying, "He saved others; he cannot save himself. Let the Messiah, the King of Israel, come down from the cross now, so that we may see and believe." Those who were crucified with him also taunted him.

The Death of Jesus

"When it was noon, darkness came over the whole land until three in the afternoon. At three o'clock Jesus cried out with a loud voice, "Eloi, Eloi, lema sabachthani?" which means, "My God, my God, why have you forsaken me?" When some of the bystanders heard it, they said, "Listen, he is calling for Elijah." And someone ran, filled a sponge with sour wine, put it on a stick, and gave it to him to drink, saying, "Wait, let us see whether Elijah will come to take him down." Then Jesus gave a loud cry and breathed his last. And the curtain of the temple was torn in two, from top to bottom. Now when the centurion, who stood facing him, saw that in this way he breathed his last, he said, "Truly this man was God's Son!"

Luke 23:39-46

"One of the criminals who were hanged there kept deriding him and saying, "Are you not the Messiah? Save yourself and us!" But the other rebuked him, saying, "Do you not fear God, since you are under the same sentence of condemnation? And we indeed have been condemned justly, for we are getting what we deserve for our deeds, but this man has done nothing wrong." Then he said, "Jesus, remember me when you come into your kingdom." He replied, "Truly I tell you, today you will be with me in Paradise."

The Death of Jesus

"It was now about noon, and darkness came over the whole land until three in the afternoon, while the sun's light failed; and the curtain of the temple was torn in two. Then Jesus, crying with a loud voice, said, "Father, into your hands I commend my spirit." Having said this, he breathed his last."

John 19:28-30

"After this, when Jesus knew that all was now finished, he said (in order to fulfill the scripture), "I am thirsty." A jar full of sour wine was standing there. So they put a sponge full of the wine on a branch of hyssop and held it to his mouth. When Jesus had received the wine, he said, "It is finished." Then he bowed his head and gave up his spirit."

It is helpful to have some commentary to help us understand the situation. Remember that Jesus is 100% man, 100% God and the human aspect of Jesus' agony is impossible for us to comprehend. The Last Supper of the night before was probably the last time that Jesus had anything to eat or drink because from the Last Supper, he went to the Garden of Gethsemane, where the arrest occurred. Nothing is recorded, but I think that Jesus did not sleep from the time he awoke on the Thursday morning until he died, a matter adding to his physical stress and weakness. His arrest in the early hours of the morning was followed by the transfer in shackles to the High Priest's place, then morning broke and the rest of the trial occurred. Times are given as 9.00am when the crucifixion started, the mention of noon and then 3.00pm in the afternoon when He died.

He was thirsty and hungry and obviously weakened because of the lack of sustenance. He was offered something for his thirst on the end of a long pole, but it is recorded that He did not drink this offering. John states this was the last thing he did while alive. For Jesus to cry out to God and ask the question "Why have you forsaken me?" is a natural human response to his physical agony. It also shows the penalty and burden of human sin that Jesus took onto his body resulted in his being shunned or forsaken by the Holy God.

The thief on the cross is an encouragement to people who think they have left their run too late to repent and turn to God. Despite anything you may have done, God assures us in 2 Peter 3:9 that He is not willing that any should perish, and we all need to come to Him in repentance and faith. If you are in this circumstance, may I suggest that the next chapter has been written for you.

There are supernatural things that occurred surrounding the time that Jesus died. Nature responded with darkness, an earthquake and bodies coming from tombs. The curtain of the temple was torn in two, symbolizing that no longer was the inner sanctum the place that only the High Priest could enter just once a year. Jesus is in the process of becoming our Great High Priest. Hardened Roman centurions were so moved they exclaimed, "Surely this man was the Son of God!" Connect this statement with Peter's Confession we read about before the disciples started their journey to Jerusalem – it had to be the Spirit of the Lord revealing this fact to the Centurion.

John's recording of Jesus' last gasp is found in John 19:30: "When Jesus had received the wine, he said, "It is finished." Then he bowed his head and gave up his spirit."

"It is finished."

It is accomplished! This is not a statement of despair, but a cry of triumph. The very thing that I came on earth to achieve, the culmination of years of detailed preparation and planning that formed God's Plan A, is accomplished. All of the promises, all of the prophecies fulfilled. The separation of a group of people descended from Abraham and Sarah into God's chosen people and the way God cared for these people is now something that, along with the Exodus from Egypt, that can be taught and spoken about to the rest of the human race.

The Agony Continues

What I am about to write about carries with it a lot of misconception and confusion. This is the reality of the subject of hell.

Is there such a place? How could God, who is supposed to be a God of love, allow such a place to exist and stand by while people suffer? Is there such a being as Satan or the Devil? How real is this being in the twenty first century?

It may surprise you to know there are more mentions of hell in the Bible than there are mentions of heaven; more descriptions that can give us some type of understanding of what hell is or what it represents. May I present my conclusion first and then work back? We have done this a few times before.

In simple terms, heaven is a place with God. Hell is a place without God.

Heaven – hell. Life – death. Light – darkness. Peace – turmoil. Calmness – Torment. Love – hatred.

With God – Without God.

As Jesus breathed his last breath, as he gave up his spirit, because the weight of the sin of the world was on him, He entered into hell. For the first time in Eternity, Jesus Christ, Son of God, Saviour, was separated from His Heavenly Father, separated from the Godhead, removed from heaven. It was not just the human death He needed to suffer but a spiritual death that alienated him from the Holy God.

What does the Bible say about hell?

I don't want to embellish this subject matter, to make it appear to be worse than it is. I don't want you who read this to think I am trying to paint a darker picture than what the Bible paints, so my intention in this short section of this book, in retracing the pathway of Jesus through His Story, is to state the verses with as little commentary as possible.

The Bible Dictionary[7] states about hell that the word derives from 'Gehenna' and the name is derived from the Hebrew 'hinnom', the valley near Jerusalem where children were sacrificed by fire in pagan rites. It was depicted as a place of unquenchable fire. The general idea of fire to express divine judgment comes from some Old Testament references. The teaching of the New Testament reinforces this belief, and I will list some of the references in a moment.

---

7 *New Bible Dictionary* Third Edition. Inter-Varsity Press, England Reprinted 2000

I wish to share with you a narrative told by Jesus that I have already mentioned in my earlier comments about the value and strength of 'Moses and the Prophets'.

The Rich Man and Lazarus (Luke 16:19-31)

"There was a rich man who was dressed in purple and fine linen and who feasted sumptuously every day. And at his gate lay a poor man named Lazarus, covered with sores, who longed to satisfy his hunger with what fell from the rich man's table; even the dogs would come and lick his sores. The poor man died and was carried away by the angels to be with Abraham. The rich man also died and was buried. In Hades, where he was being tormented, he looked up and saw Abraham far away with Lazarus by his side. He called out, 'Father Abraham, have mercy on me, and send Lazarus to dip the tip of his finger in water and cool my tongue; for I am in agony in these flames.' But Abraham said, 'Child, remember that during your lifetime you received your good things, and Lazarus in like manner evil things; but now he is comforted here, and you are in agony. Besides all this, between you and us a great chasm has been fixed, so that those who might want to pass from here to you cannot do so, and no one can cross from there to us.' He said, 'Then, father, I beg you to send him to my father's house— for I have five brothers—that he may warn them, so that they will not also come into this place of torment.' Abraham replied, 'They have Moses and the prophets; they should listen to them.' He said, 'No, father Abraham; but if someone goes to them from the dead, they will repent.' He said to him, 'If they do not listen to Moses and the prophets, neither will they be convinced even if someone rises from the dead.'"

Hades is another term for Hell. By the fact that Jesus mentioned Hades as a place where the rich man was located after death suggests such a place or situation exists. It is important to recognize that heaven, or hell, as a destination after death has nothing to do with our wealth or lack of it on earth while we are alive. The only factor that determines our fate is our attitude to Jesus. This has been mentioned previously, and I will mention this at length in the last chapter.

Some facts we can glean from this narrative.

Verse 26 clearly states there is a great chasm set in place after death that cannot be crossed. You may hear the expression "death is so final." It certainly is, so it is essential that we all make a decision now, while we are alive and while we have the time to decide whether we accept God or reject Him.

Verse 31 has already been mentioned earlier to give weight to the Bible. Friends, if you choose to take no notice of the Bible and its teachings, if you don't accept the Bible is what it says it is, Jesus affirms that even someone rising from the dead will not be enough to convince you that there is a life after death, and that God is who He says He is in the Bible.

Look at some other descriptions of Hell or Hades.

Verse 23 states that, "It is a place of torment." Verse 25 mentions agony. What greater torment could the rich man face than to see the poor man who used to sit at his gate being licked by dogs being in Abraham's bosom? The words "if only" would echo throughout Eternity in the rich man's mind.

Verse 24 mentions Hell as a place of thirst because of the flames.

In other passages from the Bible such as Jude 1:23 the reality of fire is reinforced – "save others by snatching them out of the fire; and have mercy on still others with fear, hating even the tunic defiled by their bodies."

In what seems a contrast, there is also a description of darkness. I have heard some question how you can have fire and darkness together, but we read in Matthew 25:30: "As for this worthless slave, throw him into the outer darkness, where there will be weeping and gnashing of teeth." 2 Peter 2:17 states: "These (people) are waterless springs and mists driven by a storm; for them the deepest darkness has been reserved."

Revelation 9:1-6 paints a grim and frightening picture.

The Fifth Trumpet—the Bottomless Pit

"And the fifth angel blew his trumpet, and I saw a star that had fallen from heaven to earth, and he was given the key to the shaft of the bottomless pit; he opened the shaft of the bottomless pit, and from the shaft rose smoke like the smoke of a great furnace, and the sun and the air were darkened with the smoke from the shaft. Then from the smoke came locusts on the earth, and they were given authority like the authority of scorpions of the earth. They were told not to damage the grass of the earth or any green growth or any tree, but only those people who do not have the seal of God on their foreheads. They were allowed to torture them for five months, but not to kill them, and their torture was like the torture of a scorpion when it stings someone. And in those days people will seek death but will not find it; they will long to die, but death will flee from them."

I have said that I don't want to sensationalise these readings, nor will I. Have you ever had a dream where you seem to be falling, falling, falling? The thought of a bottomless pit, or another Biblical term is an Abyss, with the combination of smoke, fire, darkness, torment all coming together is something graphic and frightening. You also hear people saying, "I wish I was dead" when they were suffering. This is the vision of the last verse above.

This is the bottom line of hell. It is separation from God for eternity. It will never end. 2 Thessalonians 1:9 states: "These will suffer the punishment of eternal destruction, separated from the presence of the Lord and from the glory of his might." Revelation 20:10 adds: "And the devil who had deceived them was thrown into the lake of fire and sulphur, where the beast and the false prophet were, and they will be tormented day and night forever and ever."

Before leaving this subject of Eternal Damnation, in simple terms, what the Bible is trying to describe is a life lived with or without God. Heaven is with God, Hell is without God. Throughout our journey leading to Jesus' "That was the Week that Was," I have constantly pointed out this choice of one thing or another. Do you remember the mention of Elijah and the Prophets of Baal? "If the Lord is God, follow Him. If Baal then follow him."

Think of this life we enjoy now. Whether we have chosen to accept God and the claims of Jesus, or even if our choice has been to reject him, God still gives life and strength to all people. We take in the air we breathe, the breath that gives us life. That comes from God, our loving relationships. For the Australian, this "mate ship" is really a reflection of the love of God. Take away God and you remove mate ship, friendship, companionship and all that goes with it. Matthew 5:45 tells us, "For he makes his sun rise on the evil and on the good, and sends rain on the righteous and on the unrighteous." It was into this Hell that Jesus descended as a part of His punishment for the sins of the world.

Please spend some personal time thinking this through.

Jesus Christ, Son of God, part of the infinite, eternal Godhead responsible for the creation of the universe and this tiny planet known as Earth, created in such a detailed way to sustain life and enable life to reproduce itself, made a covenant with the created order.

That covenant was broken, the agreed treaty had to be torn up. Yet this did not catch the all-knowing omniscient God short. He already had established a Plan A of salvation and redemption that would enable the jewel of His creation to spend the rest of Eternity in close harmony and fellowship with himself, the angelic throngs and created order.

Out of love for you and me, and all who choose to accept his new treaty, his new covenant as outlined in detail in his New Testament, Jesus paid the price for the breaking of the treaty made so long ago. That price was a brutal but voluntary death on one of the most barbaric forms of execution known to man, but it also meant paying the penalty of separation or alienation from the Holy God.

This is beautifully captured in the words of a Stewart Townend hymn "How Deep the Father's Love for us"[5] which is published here.

> How deep the Father's love for us
> How vast beyond all measure
> That He should give His only Son
> To make a wretch His treasure
>
> How great the pain of searing loss
> The Father turns His face away
> As wounds which mar the Chosen One
> Bring many sons to glory
>
> Behold the man upon a cross
> My sin upon His shoulders
> Ashamed, I hear my mocking voice
> Call out among the scoffers

It was my sin that held Him there
Until it was accomplished
His dying breath has brought me life
I know that it is finished

I will not boast in anything
No gifts, no power, no wisdom
But I will boast in Jesus Christ
His death and resurrection.

"His death and resurrection."

That brings us to our last Chapter "The Rest of Time".

CHAPTER 8

THE REST OF TIME

"It is finished," was Jesus' cry from the Cross of Calvary.

There are many religions in the world whose founding prophets reached this same stage in their life and indeed, their life was finished. Some interesting history, some beautiful teachings and sayings. Some good philosophical concepts, but still their life is finished. They had and have many followers, devotees to their creed and way of life, but still their life is finished.

Yet, when Jesus Christ, Son of God, Saviour uttered these words, He was stating that what He had planned from before the Creation of the universe was not just "finished" but the plan, God's Plan A, had been accomplished. As the TV commercial stated, "There's more!"

The Apostles, the Disciples, Jesus' family and friends and other people who witnessed the crucifixion of the three people that afternoon did not know what was to come. They were not to know the agony, torment, bottomless pit filled with smoke and fire and the sense of hopelessness that was to come at the point of death. They certainly did not know anything at all about the resurrection of this same Jesus that was to be witnessed after the Passover Sabbath had passed. They did not know that the horrible scene they had witnessed would be recorded in history as a momentous event that would start a new era in the world's calendar.

They did not know that the cross on which Jesus died would become a symbol for millions of people who were to come on Earth. They did not know that when Jesus raised Jairus' daughter or Lazarus from the dead, he was showing them that he had power and authority over death itself.

They did not know, but as we look back and read about it from over two thousand years of historic time, we have no excuse not to know.

It is accomplished!

God's perfect Plan A, the reconciliation of people to himself, has been fulfilled. Jesus has been offered once and for all as the full, perfect sacrifice for our sin.

Before moving on to "There's more", it is essential that we ensure this sacrifice Jesus paid is clearly understood. How do I benefit from the Cross? It is important, so important, that I am writing the Bible passages in the text rather than ask you to turn them up to read them. I don't want you to miss out.

It starts with Moses and the Snake in the Wilderness. (Numbers 21:4-9)

The Bronze Snake

This incident is in the closing stages of the Exodus from Egypt and follows the forty years of wandering in the desert.

"From Mount Hor they set out by the way to the Red Sea, to go around the land of Edom; but the people became impatient on the way. The people spoke against God and against Moses, "Why have you brought us up out of Egypt to die in the wilderness? For there is no food and no water, and we detest this miserable food." Then the Lord sent poisonous serpents among the people, and they bit the people, so that many Israelites died. The people came to Moses and said, "We have sinned by speaking against the Lord and against you; pray to the Lord to take away the serpents from us." So Moses prayed for the people. And the Lord said to Moses, "Make a poisonous serpent, and set it on a pole; and everyone who is bitten shall look at it and live." So Moses made a serpent of bronze, and put it upon a pole; and whenever a serpent bit someone, that person would look at the serpent of bronze and live."

Believe it or not! If you were bitten by any of the snakes, then make no mistake: you would die. The remedy seemed stupid at the time. The solution? If you were bitten, all you had to do was simply look at the pole that had been erected in the middle of the camp within sight of everyone.

Come to the New Testament to read in the Gospel of John something that connects Jesus with these snakes and Moses.

Moses Serpent (John 3:14-17)

"And just as Moses lifted up the serpent in the wilderness, so must the Son of Man be lifted up, that whoever believes in him may have eternal life. For God so loved the world that he gave his only Son, so that everyone who believes in him may not perish but may have eternal life. Indeed, God did not send the Son into the world to condemn the world, but in order that the world might be saved through him."

In his early missionary journey, the Apostle Paul fell foul of Pax Romana by casting out a demon in a girl who was used by her slave owners for telling the future. They were imprisoned by the Roman authorities because of the disturbance of the peace to await a trial the next day. We read about it in Acts 16:25-32.

Philippian Jailer

"About midnight, Paul and Silas were praying and singing hymns to God, and the prisoners were listening to them. Suddenly there was an earthquake, so violent that the foundations of the prison were shaken; and immediately all the doors were opened and everyone's chains were unfastened. When the jailer woke up and saw the prison doors wide open, he drew his sword and was about to kill himself, since he supposed that the prisoners had escaped. But Paul shouted in a loud voice, "Do not harm yourself, for we are all here." The jailer called for lights, and rushing in, he fell down trembling before Paul and Silas. Then he brought them outside and said, "Sirs, what must I do to be saved?" They answered, "Believe on the Lord Jesus, and you will be saved, you and your household." They spoke the word of the Lord to him and to all who were in his house."

Revelation 3:20 gives us an image of Jesus knocking at the door of our life, seeking an invitation to enter our life to fellowship with us. "Listen! I am standing at the door, knocking; if you hear my voice and open the door, I will come in to you and eat with you, and you with me "

I quoted Ephesians two chapters back, but it is worth repeating as we look at this situation from a slightly different perspective.

"But God, who is rich in mercy, out of the great love with which he loved us even when we were dead through our trespasses, made us alive together with Christ—by grace you have been saved— and raised us up with him and seated us with him in the heavenly places in Christ Jesus, so that in the ages to come he might show the immeasurable riches of his grace in kindness toward us in Christ Jesus. For by grace you have been saved through faith, and this is not your own doing; it is the gift of God— not the result of works, so that no one may boast. For we are what he has made us, created in Christ Jesus for good works, which God prepared beforehand to be our way of life." (Ephesians 2:4-10)

Friends, this is more than a comprehension exercise. Do you remember when we met Peter at Banias when Jesus asked the disciples who do you say that I am? Flesh and blood did not reveal the answer, but his Father who is in heaven. We need the Holy Spirit to enlighten our minds and our hearts to fully grasp what the grace of God means, what "not by works" means, and the simplicity of looking to Jesus, to put our faith in Jesus and all He has done on the Cross during that horrible of horrible days.

There is a summary and a prayer that can be prayed at the end of this book if you want to invite Jesus into your life as your Lord and Saviour. It is on page 172.

There's More

I need you to ask yourself a question: "Of what value to me, living in the twenty first century, is Jesus' resurrection?" How does it help the rest of time?

I mentioned earlier that the time of Jesus living on Earth changed the calendars and divided the historical period of time into the time before Jesus and the time after Jesus. This was BC or AD, but with changes in the world, this changed to BCE – Before the Common Era. The Bible describes the era in which we live as "The End Times." Some of the discussion you may find difficult to understand and accept, but then people would have also questioned Noah, Abraham and the Prophets of God, right up to the time of John the Baptist. Many would have greeted the prophets with skepticism, and many met Jesus with the same degree of skepticism and disbelief. That was their freedom of choice, as it is today your freedom to accept or reject what I am about to write. What I am about to write is based on the same source historically that everything else that has been written in this book – God's Word, the Bible.

All throughout the history of what we have discovered, humankind has always had the freedom to choose. We can choose to accept that God is who he says he is in the Bible, or we can reject that and follow any other pathway we choose. We can worship any god we choose, follow any teaching that strikes our fancy and resonates with us. A few chapters back, however, I took a firm, dogmatic stand to state that Jesus claims to be the only way to get to God. He stated very clearly that He was "the way, the truth and the life. No one comes to the Father except through me." (John 14:6) Earlier, in the home of Mary and Martha, when He had called following the death of his friend Lazarus, he made the claim "I am the resurrection and the life. Those who believe in me, even though they die, will live, and everyone who lives and believes in me will never die. Do you believe this?" (John 11:25 -26)

Well might I ask the same question: "Do *you* believe this?" It echoes the question Jesus asked of Simon Peter: "Who do *you* say that I am?"

Unique in all of the religions of the World that have ever been used by humankind (or likely to be used into the future) is this one fact. A fact witnessed by many and recorded in history are the words spoken by the angel of God on that early morning after the crucifixion when Mary Magdalene and the other Mary went to look at the tomb to prepare Jesus' lifeless body for a decent burial. "Do not be afraid for I know that you are looking for Jesus who was crucified. He is not here; he has risen." (Matthew 28:5-6 NIV)

He is risen!

"Where, O death, is your victory?

Where, O death, is your sting?"

The sting of death is sin, and the power of sin is the law. But thanks be to God, who gives us the victory through our Lord Jesus Christ. (1 Corinthians 15:55-57)

At this moment, and for the rest of time, you have a personal decision to make. Accept what you have read, or elect a different set of beliefs. On a personal scale, your choice will determine your manner of life, the way you choose to live and your destiny after you die.

On a larger scale, a global human scale, the same book that we have been reading that showed the culmination of numerous prophecies about Jesus Christ coming to live on Earth and to die as God's plan of salvation and redemption has made prophetic utterances about the time that it still to unfold.

The Bible tells us very clearly a number of significant global events are to occur at some time in the future.

- Jesus will return and there will be a new Heaven and a new Earth.
- There will be a Great Day of Judgment.

Friends, I wish I could tell you more than I am about to write, but two things prevent me. The advance detail is lacking in the Bible, and the detail that is there is such that I do not fully comprehend it. That may come as a surprise to you, but remember this is an average person writing a Coach Captain's commentary of the Bible. So let us scratch the surface to help us understand a little about the rest of time.

Jesus will return and there will be a New Heaven and a New Earth

Currently as I write, the media is full of argument and doomsday talk about the climate change that will bring Earth to a catastrophic end. There are projections, calculations and all types of arguments and fear being promulgated about something that will probably not happen.

From the same source of the prophecies of what became a well documented historical event when Jesus Christ lived on Earth and was crucified, come the following prophetic utterances from Jesus as recorded in Matthew 24. It is a long quote, but it is so important to ensure it is read and understood that I prefer to record it here rather than offer a reference to look up.

The Destruction of the Temple Foretold

"As Jesus came out of the temple and was going away, his disciples came to point out to him the buildings of the temple. Then he asked them, "You see all these, do you not? Truly I tell you, not one stone will be left here upon another; all will be thrown down."

Signs of the End of the Age

"When he was sitting on the Mount of Olives, the disciples came to him privately, saying, "Tell us, when will this be, and what will be the sign of your coming and of the end of the age?" Jesus answered them, "Beware that no one leads you astray. For many will come in my name, saying, 'I am the Messiah!' and they will lead many astray. And you will hear of wars and rumors of wars; see that you are not alarmed; for this must take place, but the end is not yet. For nation will rise against nation, and kingdom against kingdom, and there will be famines and earthquakes in various places: all this is but the beginning of the birth pangs."

Persecutions Foretold

"Then they will hand you over to be tortured and will put you to death, and you will be hated by all nations because of my name. Then many will fall away, and they will betray one another and hate one another. And many false prophets will arise and lead many astray. And because of the increase of lawlessness, the love of many will grow cold. But the one who endures to the end will be saved. And this good news of the kingdom will be proclaimed throughout the world, as a testimony to all the nations; and then the end will come.

The Desolating Sacrilege

"So when you see the desolating sacrilege standing in the holy place, as was spoken of by the prophet Daniel (let the reader understand), then those in Judea must flee to the mountains; the one on the housetop must not go down to take what is in the house; the one in the field must not turn back to get a coat. Woe to those who are pregnant and to those who are nursing infants in those days! Pray that your flight may not be in winter or on a sabbath. For at that time there will be great suffering, such as has not been from the beginning of the world until now, no, and never will be. And if those days had not been cut short, no one would be saved; but for the sake of the elect those days will be cut short. Then if anyone says to you, 'Look! Here is the Messiah!' or 'There he is!'—do not believe it. For false messiahs and false prophets will appear and produce great signs and omens, to lead astray, if possible, even the elect. Take note, I have told you beforehand. So, if they say to you, 'Look! He is in the wilderness,' do not go out. If they say, 'Look! He is in the inner rooms,' do not believe it. For as the lightning comes from the east and flashes as far as the west, so will be the coming of the Son of Man. Wherever the corpse is, there the vultures will gather.

The Coming of the Son of Man

"Immediately after the suffering of those days the sun will be darkened, and the moon will not give its light; the stars will fall from heaven, and the powers of heaven will be shaken.

"Then the sign of the Son of Man will appear in heaven, and then all the tribes of the earth will mourn, and they will see 'the Son of Man coming on the clouds of heaven' with power and great glory. And he will send out his angels with a loud trumpet call, and they will gather his elect from the four winds, from one end of heaven to the other.

The Lesson of the Fig Tree

"From the fig tree learn its lesson: as soon as its branch becomes tender and puts forth its leaves, you know that summer is near. So also, when you see all these things, you know that he is near, at the very gates. Truly I tell you, this generation will not pass away until all these things have taken place. Heaven and earth will pass away, but my words will not pass away.

The Necessity for Watchfulness

"But about that day and hour no one knows, neither the angels of heaven, nor the Son, but only the Father. For as the days of Noah were, so will be the coming of the Son of Man. For as in those days before the flood they were eating and drinking, marrying and giving in marriage, until the day Noah entered the ark, and they knew nothing until the flood came and swept them all away, so too will be the coming of the Son of Man. Then two will be in the field; one will be taken and one will be left. Two women will be grinding meal together; one will be taken and one will be left. Keep awake therefore, for you do not know on what day your Lord is coming. But understand this: if the owner of the house had known in what part of the night the thief was coming, he would have stayed awake and would not have let his house be broken into. Therefore you also must be ready, for the Son of Man is coming at an unexpected hour."

The following quote is taken from the last book of the Bible called The Revelation of John. The author of the Gospel of John was exiled to a small Greek island close to what is now the Turkish Coast and it is during this time of exile that he was given a special revelation from God in a deeply spiritual sense. It is not an easy book to read or understand, but it is very clear in speaking about what the Bible calls "The Last Times" and what is to come. We are living now in "The Last Times." The days from when Jesus went to heaven on a cloud after His resurrection until the time that He will return to Earth is known as the Last Times.

A New Heaven and a New Earth (Revelation 21:1-8)

"Then I saw a new heaven and a new earth; for the first heaven and the first earth had passed away, and the sea was no more. And I saw the holy city, the new Jerusalem, coming down out of heaven from God, prepared as a bride adorned for her husband. And I heard a loud voice from the throne saying,

"See, the home of God is among mortals. He will dwell with them; they will be his peoples, and God himself will be with them; he will wipe every tear from their eyes. Death will be no more; mourning and crying and pain will be no more, for the first things have passed away."

"And the one who was seated on the throne said, "See, I am making all things new." Also he said, "Write this, for these words are trustworthy and true." Then he said to me, "It is done! I am the Alpha and the Omega, the beginning and the end. To the thirsty I will give water as a gift from the spring of the water of life. Those who conquer will inherit these things, and I will be their God and they will be my children. But as for the cowardly, the faithless, the polluted, the murderers, the fornicators, the sorcerers, the idolaters, and all liars, their place will be in the lake that burns with fire and sulphur, which is the second death."

There will be a Great Day of Judgment

Hebrews 9:27 is something I have already quoted previously. "And just as it is appointed for mortals to die once, and after that the judgment," and Acts 17:31 clearly states, "Because he has fixed a day on which he will have the world judged in righteousness by a man whom he has appointed, and of this he has given assurance to all by raising him from the dead."

Revelation 20:11-15 is a graphic picture relating to what the Bible calls "The Book of Life."

The Dead Are Judged

"Then I saw a great white throne and the one who sat on it; the earth and the heaven fled from his presence, and no place was found for them. And I saw the dead, great and small, standing before the throne, and books were opened. Also another book was opened, the book of life. And the dead were judged according to their works, as recorded in the books. And the sea gave up the dead that were in it, Death and Hades gave up the dead that were in them, and all were judged according to what they had done. Then Death and Hades were thrown into the lake of fire. This is the second death, the lake of fire; and anyone whose name was not found written in the book of life was thrown into the lake of fire."

But what if you have put your faith and trust in Jesus?

In many ways, the Judgement of God, covered by the Grace of God is all lopsided and is biased towards mankind. As Creator, the author of the Covenants made with us, the Creator and Sustainer of the universe, God must have the casting vote in all of these dealings with people. It is shear arrogance to think otherwise.

Yet His Plan A (Remember initiated and instituted from before creation?) means that, " And just as Moses lifted up the serpent in the wilderness, so must the Son of Man be lifted up, that ***whoever believes in him may have eternal life***." (John 3:14-15 emphasis mine)

These are Jesus' further words of assurance from John 14:1-3

"Do not let your hearts be troubled. Believe in God, believe also in me. In my Father's house there are many dwelling places. If it were not so, would I have told you that I go to prepare a place for you? And if I go and prepare a place for you, I will come again and will take you to myself, so that where I am, there you may be also. Let not your hearts be troubled. Believe in God; believe also in me. In my Father's house are many rooms. If it were not so, would I have told you that I go to prepare a place for you? And if I go and prepare a place for you, I will come again and will take you to myself, that where I am you may be also."

Let us take heart as we read about the first Christian martyr – the Apostle Stephen. Do you remember that Jesus said that to follow Him would involve suffering and even death?

I need you to turn to your Bible to read all of Acts Chapter 6 from verse 8 through to Chapter 7:53. Stephen's speech to the Sanhedrin had to give an account of a trumped up charge against him about blasphemy. This speech is a beautiful summary of the whole history of the Jewish race from Abraham to Jesus and covers what we have covered in our walk through the Bible.

Let me conclude with the text of The Stoning of Stephen found in Acts 7 from verse 54.

The Stoning of Stephen

"When they heard these things, they became enraged and ground their teeth at Stephen. But filled with the Holy Spirit, he gazed into heaven and saw the glory of God and Jesus standing at the right hand of God. "Look," he said, "I see the heavens opened and the **Son of Man standing** at the right hand of God!" But they covered their ears, and with a loud shout all rushed together against him. Then they dragged him out of the city and began to stone him; and the witnesses laid their coats at the feet of a young man named Saul. While they were stoning Stephen, he prayed, "Lord Jesus, receive my spirit." Then he knelt down and cried out in a loud voice, "Lord, do not hold this sin against them." When he had said this, he died." (emphasis mine)

Earlier when we discussed Jesus' cry "It is finished," we read that Jesus was now sitting at the right hand of God. Stephen saw Jesus standing.

Why? Because Jesus is a gentleman and is standing to welcome Stephen into heaven! I believe that we can have an assurance that the moment we draw our final breath, we will be welcomed into Jesus' arms.

For the rest of Time

Friends, God's promise to you and to me is that we might have a life in all its fullness – an abundant life. This does not suggest a life of wealth and freedom from problems, but one where we can know we have God on our side. God's promises for us are for the here and now, as well as a future life after death.

Jesus will come again. There will be a Great Day of Judgment. There is the assurance of Eternal life with God, provided you place your faith and trust in the Lord Jesus Christ. The Bible in Galatians 3:26 to 29 assures you that you are a child of God – "So in Christ Jesus you are all children of God through faith, for all of you who were baptized into Christ have clothed yourselves with Christ. There is neither Jew nor Gentile, neither slave nor free, nor is there male and female, for you are all one in Christ Jesus. If you belong to Christ, then you are Abraham's seed, and heirs according to the promise." You have peace with God through Christ as confirmed in Romans 5:1 – "Therefore, since we are justified through faith, we have peace with God through our Lord Jesus Christ."

For the remaining days you have alive, God has promised His Holy Spirit to dwell within you to give you the inner strength to live the way He desires you to live, to direct your pathway through life and to assist you in praying to Him. Jesus' last words as He ascended to heaven after His resurrection were, "And remember, I am with you always, to the end of the age." (Matthew 28:20)

After that, for Eternity, you will be with God your creator in His new heaven and new earth with those who also have called on His name.

Echo with confidence and peaceful assurance the beautiful words of the hymn written two centuries past by a blind Christian lady, Fanny Crosby.[8]

> Blessed assurance, Jesus is mine!
> Oh, what a foretaste of glory divine!
> Heir of salvation, purchase of God,
> Born of His Spirit, washed in His blood
>
> Chorus:
> This is my story, this is my song,
> Praising my Savior all the day long;
> This is my story, this is my song,
> Praising my Savior all the day long.

The last words written in the Bible?

The one who testifies to these things says, "Surely I am coming soon."

Amen. Come, Lord Jesus!

The grace of the Lord Jesus be with all the saints. Amen. (Revelation 22:20-21)

---

8 *Blessed Assurance* – Fanny Crosby 1873 Common Domain

POSTSCRIPT – P.S.

A summary of the Gospel - the Good News of Jesus Christ.

1. We are all sinners - "since all have sinned and fall short of the glory of God." Romans 3:23

2. The penalty for sin is death - separation from God. "For the wages of sin is death." Romans 6:23

3. But from the very beginning of time, Gods plan was to cover this penalty through the voluntary death of His Son, Jesus. "But the free gift of God is eternal life in Christ Jesus our Lord." (Romans 6:23); and, "For God so loved the world that he gave his only Son, so that everyone who believes in him may not perish but have eternal life." John 3:16

4. God wants you to turn from your sin and surrender your life to Him. "While God has overlooked the times of human ignorance, now he commands all people everywhere to repent." Acts 17:30

5. Jesus is knocking on the door of your heart and awaits your invitation to become your Lord and Saviour. "Listen! I am standing at the door, knocking; if you hear my voice and open the door, I will come in to you and eat with you, and you with me." Revelation 3:20

6. The Angels of heaven (and your Christian friends) will rejoice. "Just so, I tell you, there will be more joy in heaven over one sinner who repents than over ninety-nine righteous persons who need no repentance." Luke 15:7

Pray This Prayer

Lord Jesus, I admit that I am a sinner in need of your forgiveness and salvation. I repent of my sin and express my deepest sorrow and sadness for sinning against you and against others. Please forgive me, and I pray that you will cleanse my heart and soul. Fill me with your Holy Spirit and give me the strength to go on my way to sin no more.

I invite Jesus to come into my heart and life to become Lord of my life.

Thank you for the assurances in your Word, the Bible that He is true to his promises and that he will lead and guide my life.

Amen.

If you have prayed this prayer, we all rejoice with you.

POSTSCRIPT - P.S.

It is helpful and important that you share this great news with someone you know to be a Christian person - a friend, someone at church or your minister if you attend church. Get involved with a study of God's word as soon as possible.

You are welcome to write to me at buspa@icloud.com.

John Cronshaw

OTHER BOOKS FROM JOHN CRONSHAW:

COACHED BY GOD

A great summary of how one can effectively take in God's principles and promises in all aspects of life.

BUSPA'S CORNER

A series of 31 devotions suitable for personal or group reading with many taken from experiences on the road.

MOVING DEVOTIONS (CD)

Devotions given on the road and some Australian poetry makes a very listenable CD and a great gift.

THE LAND OF THE BIBLE

A handy book to use as a guide to any sightseeing programme of the Land of the Bible.

www.ingramcontent.com/pod-product-compliance
Lightning Source LLC
LaVergne TN
LVHW051520070426
835507LV00023B/3206